The *Tarot*
Directory

Annie Lionnet

The Tarot Directory

Grange
BOOKS

Text and design copyright © The Ivy Press Limited 2004

First published in the UK in 2004 for Grange Books
an imprint of Grange Books plc
The Grange
Kingsnorth Industrial Estate
Hoo, nr Rochester
Kent ME3 9ND
www.Grangebooks.co.uk

by arrangement with THE IVY PRESS LIMITED

ISBN: 1-84013-667-7

This book was conceived, designed, and produced by
THE IVY PRESS LIMITED
The Old Candlemakers, West Street,
Lewes, East Sussex, BN7 2NZ

CREATIVE DIRECTOR Peter Bridgewater
PUBLISHER Sophie Collins
EDITORIAL DIRECTOR Steve Luck
DESIGN MANAGER Tony Seddon
DESIGNER Kevin Knight
PROJECT EDITOR Mandy Greenfield
PICTURE RESEARCH Vanessa Fletcher
STUDIO PHOTOGRAPHY Guy Ryecart

Originated and printed in China

THE WHEEL OF FORTUNE

Contents

How to use this book   6
Different decks, different influences   8

Tarot Basics   9
History and symbolism   10
Learning to trust the Tarot   12
Delving beneath the surface   14
Illuminating our inner selves   16
More decks, more influences   18

The Major Arcana   19
The Major Arcana at a glance   64

The Minor Arcana   65
Cups   66
Wands   94
Pentacles   122
Swords   150
The Minor Arcana at a glance   178

Preparing for a Reading   179
Choosing a pack   180
Setting the scene   182
Synchronicity and practice   184
Reading for a friend   186

Case Histories   187
The Celtic Cross   188
The Three-Card Spread   190
The Horoscope Spread   192
The Triangle   194
The Star Spread   196
The Consequences Spread   198
The Five-Card Horseshoe Spread   200
Creating your own spread   202

Useful websites and books   204
Index   206
Acknowledgments   208

How to use this book

The Emperor from the Golden Dawn Tarot reflects a powerful resource within us that enables us to take control of our lives.

The most common use of Tarot is for the purpose of divination—the word "divination" coming from the Latin *divinare*, meaning "to divine" or "to foresee." In this way, the Tarot is used as a means of understanding ourselves better and gleaning insights into the future. It offers us a form of guidance, whether we are asking a simple question of a practical nature or struggling with a much more complex matter. It can also help us to identify any obstacles that stand in our way and the resources that we possess to overcome them.

Illustrations show the various ways in which different decks have portrayed the same card

Symbolism describes the multiple associations of each card and what it represents

The introduction to each card gives an overview of its significance and describes different depictions

Interpretation indicates what the card in question may mean if you draw it in your spread

Tarot decks are divided into the Major Arcana (which comprises 21 numbered cards, plus the unnumbered Fool card) and the Minor Arcana (comprising 56 cards making up of four suits: Cups, Wands, Pentacles, and Swords). *The Tarot Directory* starts by looking at the history and uses of the Tarot and the ways in which it can help us. It then introduces all the cards of the Major Arcana, followed by those of the four Minor Arcana suits, and examines their symbolism and interpretations. The book ends with practical advice on preparing for a reading, case histories showing different spreads, and tips on creating your own layout.

Writing your readings down may help to clarify their significance. It is also helpful to keep a note of the spreads that you do.

The numbered diagram shows the order in which the cards should be laid out

A brief biography describes the questioner's background and why he or she is seeking a reading

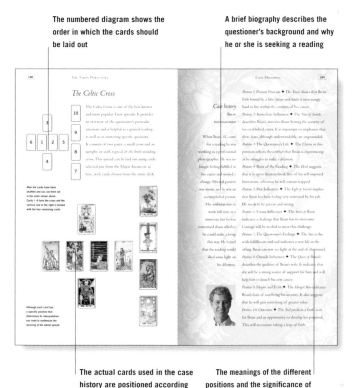

The actual cards used in the case history are positioned according to the spread in question

The meanings of the different positions and the significance of the chosen cards are explained

Different decks, different influences

Six of the decks illustrated throughout *The Tarot Directory* are shown here; the remaining six decks are illustrated on page 18.

The earliest set of Tarot cards was the Visconti-Sforza deck, produced in Italy in the mid-fifteenth century, showing heraldic symbols and religious scenes.

Today it is the Tarot de Marseilles designs, which date from the sixteenth century, that are generally accepted as standard.

The Hermetic Order of the Golden Dawn incorporated astrology and placed greater emphasis on the elements, planets, and signs of the Zodiac.

The Royal Fez Moroccan Tarot was commissioned by the founder of Mensa, Roland Berrill, in the 1950s from artist Michael Hobdell to reflect a Moroccan ambience.

Aleister Crowley extended the teachings of the Golden Dawn and reinterpreted the symbolism of the Tarot, designing his own pack, known as the Thoth deck.

The occultist Arthur Waite created a deck in 1916, of which the Universal Waite Tarot is one variation. He also made the Tarot more accessible.

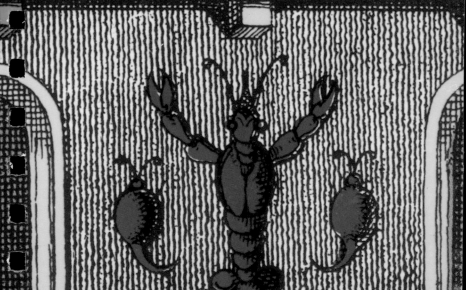

Tarot Basics

The Tarot is a way of developing our intuitive skills so that we can draw on them when we need either insight or guidance. When we consult the Tarot we are attempting to better comprehend both ourselves and the forces that are at work within our psyches and in our outer lives. The Tarot can be used not only to help us come to terms with ourselves, but to gain a greater understanding of the people who are significant in our lives. As we familiarize ourselves with the images and symbols in the decks, so we begin to become more aware of our own inner landscape.

History and symbolism

Tarot cards have existed for hundreds of years. This is the earliest known painting (dating from c.1400) of playing tarocchi.

The earliest origins of the Tarot are ambiguous and to this day they remain shrouded in mystery. One theory is that they lay in the religious rituals and symbols of the ancient Egyptians; another theory is that they derived from the Celts; yet others speculate that the Tarot was brought to Europe from elsewhere (possibly from Egypt, China, India, or Persia) by gypsies—but all of this is mere conjecture. By whom the cards were originally designed and for what exact purpose still eludes us.

What we do know is that the Tarot that we use today dates back to the mid-fifteenth century, when the aristocratic Italian Visconti-Sforza family commissioned the painting of several Tarot decks. However, in the seventeenth century the Italians stopped manufacturing cards and began importing them from France— the Tarot de Marseilles being a well-known example of a French deck. It has been highly influential on card design in subsequent centuries.

The 78-card deck has been used in many different ways during its existence, but we have evidence that it was originally employed as a card

The Lovers from the Pierpoint Morgan deck (possibly the wedding of Francesco Sforza and Bianca Maria Visconti in October 1441).

game called *tarot* in France and *tarocchi* in Italy. Over the centuries many varying decks have been designed, but the fascination in which the Tarot was held more than

500 years ago continues to this day. Self-knowledge was the first dictum of the Greeks: "Know thyself" was carved above the doorway of Apollo's temple at Delphi, and the Tarot has been used as a means of self-knowledge since its inception. However, it has also evoked fear and suspicion over the centuries—in the Middle Ages, for instance, the Church burned many sets of Tarot cards because it was strongly opposed to the pagan imagery of the decks.

Even in the twenty-first century the Tarot is still sometimes referred to as "the devil's picture-book" and regarded as something to be reviled. In some early packs the Pope and Papess cards were replaced by the High Priest and High Priestess in order to disassociate them from Roman Catholicism. But although attempts were made to discredit or even abolish the Tarot, it continued to flourish, and by the end of the eighteenth century the divinatory meaning of the cards as we know them today had become established.

The powerful symbolism of the Major Arcana reflects the principal events in our lives, whereas the cards of the Minor Arcana inform us about our circumstances and our experiences, as well as the direction in which we may be heading. The esoteric meaning of each numbered card, its masculine or feminine principle, and the elements of air, water, fire and earth that are associated with the suits of the Minor Arcana are just some of the symbolic themes in the Tarot. But exactly why it weaves such a mysterious spell over all who consult it is hard to pinpoint. Somehow the symbolism depicted in the cards evokes spontaneous feelings and insights that cannot readily be grasped by the intellect.

Learning to trust the Tarot

Nobody knows for sure how the Tarot is able to reflect our individual situation so accurately. To gain a deeper understanding of this, we need to delve into the world of the psyche, where experiences are connected by synchronicity (the meaningful coincidence of an outer event and an inner state). Many people believe that Carl Jung's "theory of synchronicity" is at work when we consult the cards. He postulated that everything in the universe is connected and that the outer world is a mirror of our inner world. Therefore the question that we ask the Tarot will be reflected in our choice of cards. When we select a card, it reflects an inner image of ourselves, which may also be mirrored in an outer situation that is prevailing at the time of the reading. Sometimes we will recognize quite easily what is being revealed; at other moments we may well be meeting an aspect of ourselves for the first time.

Developing a relationship with the Tarot takes time and patience. We need to become familiar with the coded motifs of the cards by working with them and practicing different spreads. Slowly we will begin to develop a trust in the way in which each card reveals

Carl Jung (1875–1961) devoted much of his life to studying symbolism and coined the term "synchronicity."

XXI

♄   The Universe   ♒

Everything in the universe is connected. When we experience this kind of unity, we see ourselves as part of a greater whole.

the meaning of a particular situation. We may not be able to explain exactly how this process works, but we learn from experience that the Tarot always sheds light on our circumstances and shines the way forward, if only we are willing to look and attempt to comprehend what we are being told.

Many people look to the Tarot cards for fortune-telling, which is also known as cartomancy. Although the cards are not intended to predict a fixed future—but, rather, the likely outcome of a given situation—this use of Tarot remains popular. Increasingly, however, people are becoming interested in the psychological advantages that a Tarot reading can offer.

When we use the Tarot as an aid to learning more about ourselves, we are working with the powerful symbolism of the cards, rather than with their predictive attributes. From the very beginning, humankind developed symbolic languages to describe the rich world of the unconscious. Whenever we consult the Tarot, we are given a glimpse of the psychological patterns, the spiritual aspirations, and the hidden motivations that govern our lives.

Psychology uses the word "archetypal" to describe these universal patterns that are inherent in all of us. We are "fated" to have certain experiences in life, such as the joy of getting married, or becoming a parent, or the sadness of experiencing a loss. Sometimes we embrace such an experience and at other times we try to deny or repress it. The Tarot reflects these archetypal situations and gives us insight into how to deal with them. Whatever purpose we put to the Tarot, it is important to treat it with the respect that it deserves.

Death indicates the passing of an old way of life. The skeleton is not a symbol of a literal death, but rather of transformation.

Delving beneath the surface

The Tarot reflects all the various stages of life through which we must pass. There are times for beginnings and times for endings—and for everything else in between. If we wish the Tarot to shed light on our present situation, then we need to learn the meaning of the symbols on each card, as described in the sections on the Major and Minor Arcana that follow (*pages 19–64 and pages 65–178, respectively*). The more understanding we have of their symbolism, the more the cards will be able to "speak" to us and bring what we already know to light.

The Chariot symbolizes our need for self-control, discipline, and willpower as we struggle with the conflicting forces within us.

Taken at face value, Tarot cards often draw us to their colorful and compelling imagery: ranging from the lunar symbols associated with the High Priestess to the Chariot that is being pulled in opposite directions by two different-colored horses; from the figure seen fighting a lion on the Strength card to the skeleton with a scythe that is the traditional image of Death. However, as we begin to work with the Tarot, we are drawn ever deeper into new and illuminating discoveries about ourselves. A Tarot reading can make a meaningful statement about our lives—however difficult or challenging things happen to be for us at the time in question. And it also gives us a chance to become more whole and integrated as human beings.

The Tarot cannot foretell a definite future—it is not directive and does not make decisions for us. We all possess free will, and we always have a choice as to whether or not to follow the guidance that is offered by the Tarot. However, it does indicate trends and influences that may lead to a particular conclusion and serves as a tool for greater self-awareness. It portrays a series of images that reflect the qualities of the precise time when we consult the cards with a specific problem or situation in mind.

Rather than focusing on a future that is scripted, we gain more benefit from seeing how the inner qualities and meanings of the moment are revealed through the imagery and symbolism of the cards. Many people fear the Tarot, because they believe that it describes our lives in a fated way. In reality it illustrates influences, opportunities, and aspects of ourselves that we are either unaware of or have hidden from our conscious mind. The Greeks did not believe that fate was a random or arbitrary series of events, which we are at the mercy of and which we are powerless to change. It is true that certain events in our lives have a predestined quality and appear to be written into our appointed lot. However, by and large the Greeks saw fate as a complex and infinite web of choices, each of which has a different consequence.

Often we consult the cards when we are at a turning point in our lives or have a difficult decision to make; the cards will highlight our dilemma and indicate the potential direction in which we will head. Even when our choices are necessarily limited, the Tartot can offer us guidance concerning both our present and our future.

Illuminating our inner selves

The choices we made in the past affected our present circumstances, and the choices that we make now will affect our future. Many of our choices are conscious ones, but a surprising number of them remain unconscious, until we seek a deeper awareness of our inner lives. The images embodied in the Tarot can help us connect to what is hidden from view within us.

The language of the unconscious comes to us in dreams and offers us clues to understand ourselves at a deeper level.

When we consult the cards, we seek to comprehend the patterns that underlie our lives. By understanding the influences that are at work in our psyches, we can work from a position of strength based on self-awareness.

We are only fated to struggle in the dark and repeat unwanted behavior patterns when we have little or no understanding of why we are the way we are. The Tarot is a powerful tool for reaching deep into our inner landscape and illuminating whatever is ready to be revealed.

In much the same way as dreams speak to us, the Tarot directly addresses the unconscious —only through pictures rather than words. All we have to do is allow ourselves to learn its language, by familiarizing ourselves with the various images, their symbolism, and their differing interpretations. Tarot cards do not offer a "right" and "wrong" interpretation;

Each Tarot picture resonates with the contents of our unconscious, which is activated by these powerful images.

in fact, they may have dual (and sometimes even apparently contradictory) meanings, depending on the person and the circumstances to which they are referring. It is a question of using the explanation that is most apt for your own situation.

Unless we have some understanding of the psyche, the seemingly strange coincidences that occur in our readings can make us feel afraid or uneasy. Although we are often concerned with the way that a particular situation will turn out, it is usually more helpful to understand the rhythms and patterns at work, so that we can cooperate with our circumstances rather than fight against them. If we work with the guidance offered by the Tarot, we are more likely to effect a positive outcome—or, at the very least, bring a greater understanding to our situation.

The images of the Tarot sometimes reveal themselves to us immediately, but more often it takes time to interpret their symbolism and what they have to say to us. Each card has an archetypal meaning that mirrors all of the various aspects of human existence. When we consult the Tarot, we choose the exact cards that reflect our particular experience at the time of the reading. If the Tarot works in a predictive sense, it is because it is a mirror of the psyche and reveals things that could never be discovered using our rational intellect. The Tarot can be remarkably accurate and perceptive. Some people believe this is because there is a higher intelligence at work, which in some way directs the shuffling and selection of the cards, so that the exact images that give an answer to our problem appear in just the right order.

More decks, more influences

Six of the decks illustrated throughout *The Tarot Directory* are shown here; the remaining six decks are illustrated on page 8.

The Medieval Scapini Tarot recreates through its images (which incorporate hidden clues) the magnificence of the Middle Ages and Renaissance.

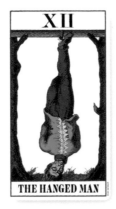

The Swiss 1JJ Tarot dates from the mid-seventeenth century. JJ refers to the old cards of Juno and Jupiter, whose names were changed to appease the Church.

Each card of the Herbal Tarot depicts a different named herb and the symbolism of the pack incorporates their long-established healing powers.

Russian artist Yury Shakov designed the oval-shaped miniatures of Russian folk and fairy tales that feature on the Russian Tarot of St. Petersburg.

The Morgan Greer deck uses beautifully rich colors. It draws much of its imagery from the Rider-Waite pack, although its figures are more striking.

Zolar's Astrological Tarot is a classic deck using a standardized color code of green and pink. It was designed by Zolar, based on the Rider-Waite deck.

The Major Arcana

The 22 trumps of the Major Arcana describe the archetypal stages of life that all of us experience. The Fool, which is unnumbered, specifically represents the beginning of this journey. The 21 numbered cards that follow describe different aspects of the questioner and other personalities who are met along the way. The Major Arcana also describes situations we will encounter and qualities we will need in order to deal with them. Its images are very powerful, because they describe significant turning points in our lives and reflect important psychological processes, as well as untapped potential.

The Fool

The Fool walks toward the right of the picture, indicating the development of consciousness

The dog depicts instinctive forces in the unconscious that are ready to help or warn us

THE FOOL

START OF A PHASE ☾ LEAP OF FAITH ☾ OPENNESS TO LIFE

MARSEILLES TAROT

The Fool is the only card in the Major Arcana that also exists in the modern playing cards that we use today. He is the joker in the pack, the "wild card" who does not adhere to the rules and who flaunts convention. In the Tarot the Fool is the unnumbered card that does not fit into an ordered sequence. He represents the free-spirited side of our nature—the maverick in us who refuses to toe the line and conform to people's expectations. He is often depicted as a court jester or the divine fool, but is in fact an ambivalent figure.

Symbolism

The Fool is often portrayed as a carefree and apparently innocent young man whose next step will take him over the edge of a cliff. He represents the beginning of a new chapter, but for this to occur a willingness to make a leap of faith is needed, which does necessitate taking a risk. Old habits have become outdated and no longer foster our growth. Sometimes this is a conscious process, but as often as not something happens to remind us that we have outgrown a phase of our lives. To deny the call to adventure can result in a stifling of our creativity and spirit, and the desire for new experiences is a powerful motivating force. Such a strong impetus for change may appear foolhardy to others; nevertheless, the anticipation of untold future possibilities is what compels us to move forward. Ultimately the Fool is our innate desire to develop our full potential and keeps us from stagnating.

Interpretation

If the Fool appears in a reading, it suggests that unexpected opportunities may be just around the corner and the challenge to meet these is stronger than your fear of the unknown. There is an inherent capacity to trust the path and a willingness to take your chances, regardless of the outcome. It's a case of nothing ventured, nothing gained. This card offers a sense that everything is full of promise. You are at the beginning of a new cycle of self-discovery and, however precarious it may seem, you feel compelled to follow your intuition. When you choose the Fool, you are being given the chance to adopt a more open attitude to life. You are willing to abandon your need for security and trust that whatever you experience will be worthwhile and meaningful. A new way of life is possible as you begin to feel renewed energy and a commitment to moving forward.

Medieval Scapini Tarot

The Magician

I

The energy embodied in the Magician is actively directed toward realizing our potential

The Magician represents our capacity for self-realization

כ   The Magician   ☿

GUIDANCE (NEW OPPORTUNITIES (CREATIVE INITIATIVE

THOTH TAROT

The Magician is the first numbered card of the Major Arcana, and "one" is the number of masculine power, which is forceful and decisive and able to initiate new beginnings. In many Tarot decks the Magician is depicted with a lemniscate, the mathematical symbol for infinity, above his head. He can be a manipulator and even a trickster and exemplifies the creative power of the intellect, which can be ᵍed both positively and negatively. The Magician is simultaneously ᵗʰer and guide and offers the gift of knowledge and learning.

Symbolism

The Magician is associated with the Greek messenger-god Hermes, who acted as a mediator between the divine and human realms, and symbolizes the link between the conscious and the unconscious mind. The Magician is often depicted with one arm raised and the other pointing downward toward a wand, a pentacle, a sword, and a cup, illustrating his ability to draw mental and spiritual energy from above and channel it into the mundane world below. The wand, pentacle, sword, and cup of the Minor Arcana are associated with the four astrological elements—fire, earth, air, and water—as well as the four Jungian psychological functions of intuition, sensation, thinking, and feeling. They reflect our innate resources and the infinite number of possibilities that we all possess. The Magician in turn reflects our potential for self-awareness and our ability to recognize, develop and channel our abilities in a very concrete and practical way.

Interpretation

Choosing this card indicate are about to undergo an impo beginning. You are ready to dem your creative gifts and abilities and develop any untapped potential of which you may not yet be aware. This is a time for decision-making and action. A huge reservoir of power and energy is available for both creative and intellectual pursuits. Opportunities that require a focused mind and intuitive insight are likely to present themselves, giving you the chance to develop your skills. You have not only the mental capacity and imagination to conjure up ideas and make plans, but also the ability to translate these into action. It is time to connect with all of the resources symbolized by the four suits and promote yourself. Selecting the Magician means there are choices to be made, and you must be determined and decisive if you are to use your talents to the full.

**Pierpont Morgan
Visconti-Sforza Tarot**

The High Priestess

ie pomegranates connect the High Priestess to Persephone, Greek goddess of the Underworld, and allude to hidden riches in the unconscious mind

The horned headdress suggests a connection with the Egyptian goddess, Isis

ESOTERIC KNOWLEDGE ❨ INTUITION ❨ WISDOM

UNIVERSAL WAITE TAROT

The High Priestess is also known as the Female Pope and can be seen dressed in papal robes in the Marseilles deck. She is associated with the number two, symbolizing duality and balance as well as the polarity of opposing forces. The many lunar images portrayed in this card, such as the crescent moon in the Waite deck, demonstrate her strong connection with the moon. Her crown signifies the three phases of the moon, with the circle in the center as the full moon and the waxing and waning moon on either side.

Symbolism

The rich world of the unconscious is represented by this card. Everything is full of potential and yet hidden from view, and only time will reveal the secrets behind the veil. The High Priestess guards the mysteries of life and is often depicted holding a book or scroll symbolizing hidden truths that are yet to be revealed. She represents our need to internalize and is the energy that connects us with a deeper esoteric knowledge. In order to access her secrets we need to be receptive and adopt a meditative serenity. A period of gestation may be necessary for new life to be formed and brought to light. We need to go beyond our everyday awareness and plumb the hidden depths of our inner landscape in order to discover greater wisdom and understanding. The High Priestess symbolizes the nurturing of spiritual wisdom and knowledge and indicates that our potential needs to be brought to light. She represents the feminine power of insight, which acts as a guide to our deepest self. Through silence and contemplation we catch a glimpse of something that we may not be able to put into words, but which we intuitively understand.

Interpretation

Choosing this card indicates that you have a need for stillness and withdrawal. You are being asked to spend time looking within, rather than searching for answers outside of yourself. You may develop an interest in the occult and embark on a course of esoteric studies. You have a strong desire to learn more about what lies deep inside you, although nothing will be revealed before the fullness of time. Whether you are aware of it or not, you are in a gestation process and much growth is occurring, the major part of which is unseen. It may seem as if you are standing still, but understand that you are developing on an inner level. Outer activities now take a back seat as you attune yourself to your inner world and allow yourself to be guided by your intuition.

Marseilles Tarot

THE HIGH PRIESTESS

The Empress

She holds a scepter symbolizing her supreme power as a woman in her own right

The Empress indicates emotional fulfillment and an enjoyment of life

The Empress

ABUNDANCE ☾ FERTILITY ☾ RECEPTIVITY

RUSSIAN TAROT OF ST. PETERSBURG

The Empress is often portrayed as a woman who is content and at peace with herself. The robes that she wears allude to the fact that she might be pregnant. Her number is three, representing the bringing together of opposites to create something new. Some packs depict her standing in a field of corn or wheat that is ready to be harvested. She is the personification of fruitfulness and abundance and represents the cycles of nature, from birth to death. She also embodies an earthy, physical sensuality and nurturing of the body.

Symbolism

The Empress is the symbol of fertility and new life. She embodies the dual aspects of motherhood—the joy of giving birth to a child and the mourning of the inevitable separation that is inherent in being a mother. The fact that she is often depicted in a beautiful, fertile environment surrounded by nature's bounty denotes her fecundity and the creative power of the feminine. Demeter, the grain-goddess, is one of the many mythological figures with whom the Empress is associated, underlining the theme of abundance. Both marriage and motherhood are symbolized by this card and may indicate the birth of a child or a new creative project. In both cases, devotion and careful nurturing are required to bring them to fruition. Domestic stability, protection, and maternal care are all characteristics of the Empress. This card indicates a strong sense of well-being, physical security, and emotional fulfillment. We are able to surrender and flow with the rhythm of life, as well as secure a solid foundation for our future growth. A passionate and deep love of life is reflected in the Empress, as well as a feeling of being able to "just be."

Interpretation

Choosing this card indicates that the time has come for a renewal of your circumstances. The moment is ripe to channel your energies in a creative direction and come up with new ideas for the future. The upsurge of creativity depicted by the Empress needs a concrete outlet if you are to realize your innate potential. Look for practical ways in which you can express this strong sense of wanting to expand your life. You are able to give and receive now in equal measure and to enjoy the harmony and love that surround you. This card indicates the emotional fulfillment that you feel when you are in a happy, secure relationship that is nurturing and life-sustaining and gives you room to grow. It is time to enjoy your creativity and make the most of your talents.

Golden Dawn Tarot

3 THE EMPRESS

The Emperor

The Emperor wears a golden eagle crown linking him to Zeus, the ruler of the gods

IV — THE EMPEROR

Material wealth and inner strength are symbolized by the golden clasp of his rich cloak and by his armor

AMBITION ☾ AUTHORITY ☾ WORLDLY SUCCESS

MORGAN GREER TAROT

The Emperor and Empress form a pair. She is receptive and nurturing and represents the female aspect, whereas he is dynamic and extrovert and represents the male side of nature. In most decks the Emperor is shown seated on a throne, dressed in formal robes. He holds an orb and scepter indicating his authority and power and is indicative of the desire to take control of life. He is associated with the number four, which symbolizes form, solidity, and the ability to organize and structure thoughts in a concrete way.

Symbolism

The Emperor is skilled in manifesting creative ideas and transforming them into something tangible and workable. He represents our ability to handle the material side of life and create order out of chaos. He expresses a strong yang energy, which enables us to take control of situations and use our power to realize our goals. His dignified authority commands respect and admiration. He is down-to-earth and takes life seriously, and is able to focus on his objectives to the exclusion of everything else. The Emperor represents our ability to analyze and think rationally. He is a dynamic force signifying our ambition, our drive for status and power, and material wealth. Direct, forceful, and firm, he is able to act, make tough decisions, and follow through on his word. He reflects our need to set boundaries and work within a structure; he represents our moral conduct and the code by which we live our lives. The Emperor can also manifest negatively, behaving in a rigid and judgmental way and holding impossibly high expectations, both of himself and of others.

Interpretation

Choosing this card signifies that it is time to have the courage of your convictions and play an active role in organizing matters. You are called upon to use your intellectual and reasoning skills and make decisions that you have considered carefully. Taking control of your situation puts you in a position of power and will enable you to direct the course of your life. You can translate your dreams into reality, if you are able to take personal responsibility for this process. Worldly gain and achievement are important to you now, and you may have the opportunity to start a new business or establish a home. You are willing to work hard in order to establish a solid foundation to your life. The Emperor could also signify an influential authority figure, mentor, or hard taskmaster.

Swiss 1JJ Tarot

The Hierophant

The Hierophant
strengthens our morals
and our confidence in
life and in ourselves

The search for
meaning through
religion, philosophy,
or spirituality is
indicated by this card

SPIRITUAL PURPOSE ❨ SELF-DISCOVERY ❨ INNER WISDOM
PIERPONT MORGAN VISCONTI-SFORZA TAROT

The Hierophant, or Pope as he is sometimes known, often appears
in papal robes standing between two pillars, which represent his ability
to balance opposing forces. Where the Emperor signifies the worldly
masculine, the Hierophant stands for the spiritual masculine.

He is associated with the number five, which indicates spiritual
power, inner wisdom, and mental inspiration, as well as the capacity
to synthesize information. He offers us guidance on spiritual matters
and represents the need to find a spiritual meaning to our lives.

Symbolism

The Hierophant represents the spiritual guide within each of us that links our worldly persona with our higher spiritual nature. In this way he helps us to establish a dialog between our conscious mind and the part of us that seeks to communicate with our source. In the past the old word for priest was *pontifex*, meaning "maker of bridges." His role was to create a link between people and the divine. The Hierophant reflects our inner desire to give meaning to things and to raise our consciousness so that we no longer feel divided within ourselves. The longing to experience this higher dimension of life is what Carl Jung called "the religious function." It describes the intuitive feeling that there is more to life than the simple and mundane. The Hierophant is the driving force behind the spiritual beliefs or philosophical values that each of us forms. Sooner or later, life requires us to put these to the test and see if they are able to sustain us. Ultimately, the Hierophant symbolizes our innate desire to achieve a balance between our worldly and spiritual impulses so that we become whole.

Interpretation

Drawing this card means that you are ready to experience life in a different way. It is time to turn your attention to spiritual matters and find the real meaning and purpose of your life, as you search for a deeper understanding of where you fit into the scheme of things. You may make a connection with a spiritual mentor such as a priest, or with a psychotherapist, who is able to offer you guidance and act as a catalyst in this process. On the other hand, you may embark on a course of study of a philosophical or religious nature in order to acquire a deeper knowledge of yourself. Becoming more spiritually aware will enable you to progress further while at the same time affording you greater peace of mind.

Thoth Tarot

The Hierophant

The Lovers

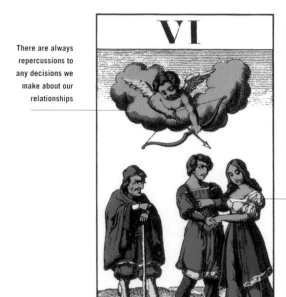

There are always repercussions to any decisions we make about our relationships

The Lovers highlights the difficulty inherent in making significant choices—particularly in love

A CHOICE ☾ SACRIFICE ☾ THE TESTING OF A RELATIONSHIP
SWISS 1JJ TAROT

The Lovers are often represented as a young man caught in the dilemma of choosing between two women. The Judgment of Paris is often linked to this card: in Greek myth, Paris had to choose which of three goddesses was the most beautiful; ultimately his choice led to the Trojan War, and his example warns of the dangers, pitfalls, and consequences of the choices that we make. Such choices are not always to do with love and romance, but nevertheless will be of enormous importance to us. This card is associated with six, the number of harmony.

Symbolism

Sooner or later we are all faced with making significant choices in our lives. Often our desire to enter a relationship represents an attempt to unite the opposites within us and to know ourselves better through being with another. The parts of ourselves that we deny or repress, or are simply unaware of—be they positive or negative—are often mirrored in our partners. When these unknown aspects of our nature are reflected back to us, we have an opportunity to integrate them and become more whole. Such increased self-awareness equips us to take responsibility for our decisions. The Lovers suggests that choices should not be made lightly, as there is often more at stake than we realize. Complications arise when decisions are made without conscious awareness of what motivates us to select one thing over another. Sometimes this card refers to a choice between a spiritual path and sexual passion, or between intuition and reason. Once a decision has been made, the pattern of our lives will change irrevocably.

Interpretation

When you pick the Lovers, your choices are likely to be put to the test. You may be about to start an important relationship, or there may be a decision to make about an existing one. You may be in two minds about an emotional commitment, or you may have to choose between love and passion or security and stability. One half of you wants to follow your heart while the other half is determined to follow your head. You may feel torn and unsure as to what direction to take. One course of action inevitably implies that something has to be left behind, in spite of the fact that it may seem equally appealing. Careful consideration of what you stand to gain and lose is required before you make a final decision. The positive meaning of this card is that, through meeting the challenges inherent in any relationship, you will ultimately learn more about yourself.

Morgan Greer Tarot

VI — THE LOVERS

The Chariot

The charioteer needs to steer a middle path between his opposing thoughts and feelings

Two sphinxes, one black and one white, draw the Chariot, symbolizing the dilemma the charioteer must solve

THE CHARIOT.

CONFLICT ❨ INTERNAL STRUGGLE ❨ POTENTIAL FOR RESOLUTION
UNIVERSAL WAITE TAROT

The Chariot is generally portrayed as a man driving a chariot that is being pulled in opposite directions by two different-colored horses. It is associated with the number seven—the number of movement, progress, and victory. These are only achieved, however, once we have overcome certain difficulties and learned to control the conflicting forces competing for supremacy within us. The Greek philosopher Plato used the idea of the charioteer and horses as a metaphor for the soul, with the black horse representing our base instincts and the white horse our better nature.

Symbolism

The horses in this card signify the contradictions and conflicts with which we do battle in our psyches. The role of the charioteer is to hold the horses together. In the same way, we can use our will and the force of our personality to handle difficult situations. This does not necessarily mean that we have total control, but if we have a strong ego, we are able to confront and master our unconscious drives and impulses. The Chariot reflects the power of our unconscious needs and the importance of knowing how to direct them in a purposeful and positive way. Ultimately this card is asking us to take up the reins and understand what is driving us, in such a way that we neither repress these powerful instincts nor give them total control. Steering a middle ground through our opposing feelings, desires and thoughts—and not acting out one extreme or another—can strengthen the ego and foster growth and change. The Chariot reminds us that conflict, provided it is handled with strength and awareness, can be a creative force for change in our lives and can prevent us from stagnating.

Interpretation

When the Chariot appears in a spread, it indicates that you have the energy to pursue a desired goal and fight for what is important to you. You may be locked in a struggle or have a conflict of interests that you cannot easily resolve, but this card indicates that you have the confidence and belief in yourself to find potential solutions. Your ambition, determination, and drive will enable you to overcome any obstacles. However, you will need to be disciplined in your approach to difficulties and stay in tune with your inner wisdom. Otherwise you could act in an overly forceful manner, simply to get your own way. Whether the conflicts are within you or with others, the Chariot indicates that you are able to cope and have the ability, self-assertion, and skill to succeed.

Marseilles Tarot

Justice

The figure of Justice holds a sword in her right hand, signifying truth and the ability to reach a just solution

The evenly balanced scales stand for the need to weigh things up before making a decision

BALANCE (WISDOM (FAIRNESS
ROYAL FEZ MOROCCAN TAROT

Justice represents the first of the four moral lessons, the others being Temperance, Strength, and the Hermit. The traditional image depicts a figure holding a pair of scales and a sword. The wise Greek goddess, Athene, is often linked with the Justice card; she used her powerful intellect and rational mind both in battle and to judge difficult situations. The concept of true justice based on fairness and reason may seem more of an ideal than a reality. Nevertheless, as human beings we still strive to uphold its principle.

Symbolism

The sword is a symbol of masculine energy, whereas the scales are representative of the feminine principle. These two images reflect the balance between male and female. Fairness and impartiality can be cold and unfeeling, unless they are tempered with compassion. The sword of discrimination enables us to cut through our prejudices and analyze a situation rationally and intelligently. The scales offer us a balanced perspective so that we are in a position to make a sound judgment, and Justice reflects our mental ability to discriminate and make dispassionate evaluations. If a situation requires an impersonal decision, then we must first weigh everything up and not be swayed by emotion or bias. This card asks us whether we are able to be honest and truthful with ourselves and accept the situation in which we find ourselves. We need to recognize that where we find ourselves is often the result of a balance between our own actions and the circumstances that life has engendered. If we can be quite honest about this and not put the blame on other people, then we will be able to move on and not get stuck in resentment and denial.

Interpretation

Justice implies that you need to weigh things rationally in order to find a fair solution. If you are involved in a legal battle, it suggests that agreement may be reached through negotiation. You need to adopt a balanced outlook and look for effective strategies to resolve your current difficulties. You have a chance to gain a clearer understanding of yourself, if you are willing to assess your situation objectively. This card requires you to analyze your position fairly and decipher where your role lies. You may be given good advice, which you need to consider carefully before acting upon. It is time to make decisions and, even though the outcome may not be what you hoped for, this card suggests that it will nevertheless be a just one.

Zolar's
Astrological
Tarot

Success in business and legal matters. Good judgment.

XI

MAJOR ARCANA

KEY 11 — JUSTICE

Injustice, legal complications. A great disappointment.

The Hermit

The lighted lantern illuminates the depths of our inner being

The Hermit is the teacher who offers us profound insights and guidance

PATIENCE ☾ SOLITUDE ☾ REFLECTION

MEDIEVAL SCAPINI TAROT

The image most commonly depicted on this card is that of an old man carrying a staff and lantern. He has learned wisdom and patience through the passage of time and is able to stand alone without feeling lonely. He is connected with the Jungian archetype of the *senex*, or wise old man, and with the Greek god Cronus, and represents one of the four moral lessons. Drawing on his own inner resources, the Hermit does not depend on others to support him, but can rely on himself. He has earned the precious gift of peace and contentment within himself.

Symbolism

The lantern of knowledge carried by the Hermit illuminates our inner life. He reflects the spiritual quest that we embark upon when we are searching for inner truths. Contemplation, meditation, and reflection are some of the paths that connect us with our deeper selves. Spending time by ourselves may lead us to the realization that we are all ultimately alone and that accepting this can help us to face our own mortality. The Hermit sometimes implies enforced limitations in our lives and circumstances that only time—and not the will—can change. Through reconciling ourselves to this reality and acquiring the wisdom not to struggle with what we cannot change, we acquire a certain humility and calm acceptance. These are important qualities, for without them the ups and downs of life would prove unmanageable. The Hermit teaches us to trust that things will change when the time is right. Nothing can be forced; we can only wait in silence and be guided by that small voice within. The Hermit may indicate that a wise teacher will come into our lives to help us connect with our inner wisdom.

Interpretation

The Hermit in a reading indicates that the time is ripe for you to embark on a period of soul-searching. This may necessitate isolation from the busyness of the outside world so that you can familiarize yourself with your inner landscape. You may embark on a course of meditation and learn how to empty your thoughts and find inner stillness. Being alone can be an uncomfortable experience, but it is a necessary one if you are to develop your own resources. Choosing this card means that you are being given the chance to examine yourself and delve into the parts that have been hidden from view. There is a strong desire to develop into a self-sufficient person in your own right. You may need to leave something behind, in order to be on your own and have the space to reassess your life.

Royal Fez Moroccan Tarot

The Wheel of Fortune

The wheel is forever turning and we do not know what life will bring

The Wheel of Fortune reminds us that we are ultimately responsible for our own fate

THE WHEEL OF FORTUNE

ENDINGS AND BEGINNINGS (A CHANGE OF CIRCUMSTANCE
MARSEILLES TAROT

The Wheel of Fortune signifies the completion of one cycle and the beginning of another. It is often portrayed as a turning wheel, with all kind of objects and people attached to it. The wheel is in perpetual motion and serves as a constant reminder that everything passes and nothing lasts for ever. Ultimately, there is little point in becoming attached to any one experience because everything is ephemeral. We are all subjected to the laws of nature as we move through our lives from birth to death.

Symbolism

This card addresses the age-old debate of fate versus free will. The Wheel of Fortune does not mean that everything in our lives is preordained, but it does remind us that we do not have total control over the outer circumstances of our lives. We are often tempted to blame fate rather than take responsibility for our lives, but this card reminds us that we all have choices, regardless of what life brings us. At a deeper level, it suggests that ultimately we are architects of our own fate, in spite of the fact that we rail against what we do not consciously choose. We may not be able to control the way in which the wheel turns, but we can control the manner in which we respond. In the Wheel of Fortune we come to see that there is a connection between what happens to us in the outside world and our own inner dynamic. If we can understand our involvement with the process and situations in which we find ourselves, then we are less likely to feel at the mercy of fate and more able to direct the course of our own lives.

Interpretation

This card heralds a fresh start. You are embarking on a new chapter and it is up to you to determine whether this will be a positive or negative experience. There may be a turn of events that you could not have predicted and over which you have little control, or an important decision to make—the more in touch you are with your capacity to make choices, the more empowered you will be. The Wheel of Fortune is reminding you that change is inevitable, for without it life would stagnate and you would cease to grow and develop your potential. You may be at a point where it is necessary to go down, in order to come up again. On the other hand, there may be a very positive momentum in your life, which enables you to let go of the past and move forward.

Universal Waite Tarot

Strength

Strength reflects our need to channel our desires toward something positive

Courage, strength, and determination are needed to face and make a relationship with our "inner lion"

8   STRENGTH

COURAGE ❈ SELF-CONFIDENCE ❈ INNER RESOURCES

GOLDEN DAWN TAROT

There has been some debate about the numbering of this card.
In some Tarot decks Strength (which is one of the four moral lessons)
is numbered eight and Justice eleven, while more modern packs have
it the other way round. Strength is often depicted as a man or woman
grappling with a ferocious lion. Containing the savage beast within us
and channeling our passionate nature positively (rather than negatively) is
the message of this card. It is up to us whether we choose
to act creatively or destructively.

Symbolism

The lion on this card signifies the power of our instinctual nature and desires. He is a symbol of the destructive urges within the psyche, but also represents our innate dignity and nobility. Strength illustrates the impulse to connect with the conflicting forces within us that we experience in the Chariot, so that we can learn to recognize and manage them. Repressing or denying these aspects of ourselves, as well as letting them run amok, can be destructive. Ideally, we find a balance by channeling the energy of these passions into positive and creative activities. Strength suggests that it is only by integrating these unconscious impulses that we can become more aware and develop a greater sense of self. On a positive level, Strength offers the opportunity for reconciliation with whatever operates destructively in our lives—whether within or without. Negatively, it reflects what happens when we are in the grip of unhealthy impulses or allow ourselves to abuse our power. We learn that, paradoxically, connecting with our less acceptable traits, such as anger and egotism, strengthens our sense of self rather than diminishing it.

Interpretation

Choosing this card is representative of the strength and courage that you need to achieve self-mastery. By using your willpower, you are able to overcome obstacles and learn self-control. If you are determined to succeed, you must have the confidence to cope with such challenges. This card suggests that you have the inner strength to face problems, but that you need to develop trust in your abilities. It is important that you confront any self-defeating traits and take positive action to lessen their negative impact on your life. Fortunately you have the staying power to persevere until you achieve your desired result. Recognize that you are equipped to deal with your powerful emotions and find a legitimate outlet for them. Once you are able to harness these energies, you will be able to express them creatively.

Herbal Tarot

The Hanged Man

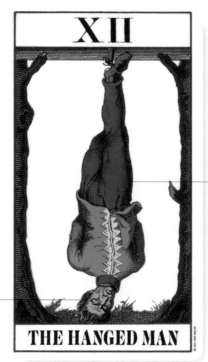

The Hanged Man signifies a turning point, perhaps toward a more spiritual life

Although being suspended by one foot looks uncomfortable, the Hanged Man copes well with hanging in this position

SACRIFICE ◖ TRANSITION ◖ SPIRITUAL TRANSFORMATION

SWISS 1JJ TAROT

The Hanged Man is frequently portrayed as a man hanging upside-down by one foot. He wears a calm and peaceful expression. In some decks, coins are falling out of his pocket, signifying the surrender of material things. The concept of giving up all worldly possessions in order to follow a spiritual path is the central theme of this card. It is worth noting that this sacrifice is voluntary and is made because what is gained is of greater value than what is lost. The inner knowledge that is acquired will be worth the sacrifice.

Symbolism

The Hanged Man symbolizes the giving up of something in order to acquire something else that has become more important. We have reached a crossroads and now we need to choose what is significant to us and what is no longer of value. This card represents a turning point in our psychological development as we reorientate our focus toward the inner world. Knowledge of what lies within becomes more important than what exists outside. The Hanged Man denotes a time when we are asked to surrender control of the ego and move into the unknown territory of our inner landscape. This necessitates a willingness to let go and trust that there is something greater than our conscious mind, which has the wisdom to guide us toward what is required for our development. Like the man hanging upside-down on the card, we need to adopt a new perspective and discover a deeper set of values within us. Whether we are aware of it or not, this card suggests that we are undergoing an expansion of consciousness that can only take place if we are ready and willing to move beyond our present set of circumstances.

Interpretation

This card in a spread signifies that you are in a state of limbo. A reorientation is taking place in your life and, for the time being at least, you may be feeling at a loss as to how to proceed. As a result you may feel in a rut and fearful. You may have no choice other than to stay where you are and await the changes that will release you from this state of stasis. You may be required to make a sacrifice in order to move forward and develop. Outworn patterns fall away and give you a new perspective on your situation. Circumstances may conspire to prevent you from focusing on your day-to-day activities for a while, so that you can concentrate on what is important. Trusting life to take its proper course will give you a sense of peace.

Morgan Greer Tarot

Death

Death, although feared, brings a new beginning

A complete transformation is possible, once the past has been relinquished

XIII

Death

ENDINGS (REBIRTH (TRANSFORMATION
THOTH TAROT

Numerous versions of this card depict Death as a skeleton carrying a scythe, the symbol of the Grim Reaper. Many people fear this card and assume that it has a literal significance. But rather than a physical death, this card is far more likely to indicate sweeping changes and the end of a particular cycle in your life. Ultimately, Death signifies that something has run its course and that a new order is ready to be implemented. How we respond to this card will largely depend on how willing we are to let go of the old and embrace the new.

Symbolism

Everything in nature is subject to cycles of death and renewal. The skeleton in this card is not a symbol of death but rather one of transformation. It serves as a stark reminder that everything that has outlived its purpose must eventually be discarded. Often we hold onto situations that hinder our growth and prevent us from moving onto the next stage of life. This card marks the transition from one state to another—such as from adolescence to adulthood, or from marriage to divorce—and signifies the conclusion of one phase and the start of another. Beginnings and endings are an inevitable part of life, and Death reminds us that we have to let something die before we can give birth to the new. This process sometimes necessitates a period of mourning, as we come to terms with what is passing out of our lives. How painful this will be is determined by our ability to surrender to the inevitability of change. Although a sense of sadness often accompanies the realization that all must pass, Death reminds us that a rebirth always follows an ending.

Interpretation

When you choose this card, you are being shown that something has reached a conclusion. You may now have to let go of what is familiar and step into the unknown. Psychological patterns that no longer serve your growth need to be relinquished, for clinging to these will only bring stagnation. You are going through radical change and, even though this may be a cause for celebration, it still requires a major adaptation on your part. You may be afraid of what the future holds and attempt to stay where you are. However, the message of this card is to permit your sense of loss, while at the same time embracing the new opportunities that the future will bring. Part of your old self has to die if you are to be transformed, and you need to trust in what lies ahead.

Golden Dawn Tarot

13 DEATH

Temperance

XIV — TEMPERANCE

The androgynous figure of this card symbolizes the reconciliation of opposites

Temperance has one foot dipped in the pool and the other on dry land, indicating the bridge between mind and body

COOPERATION (COMPROMISE (MODERATION
MORGAN GREER TAROT

A woman pouring liquid from one cup to another is the most common image to be represented on this card. Frequently one cup is gold, signifying the conscious, while the other is silver, signifying the unconscious. This image reflects the importance of a constant flow of liquid between the two, and the mixing and blending of opposites in order to find the right balance. Temperance is one of the four moral lessons to be symbolized in the Major Arcana, alongside Justice, Strength, and the Hermit.

Symbolism

Temperance is the card that denotes balanced emotions and the potential for a happy relationship. There is a strong desire to reconcile opposites and create a feeling of harmony. The Latin word *temperare*, meaning "to combine properly," describes the essence of Temperance and is symbolized by the pouring of water from one cup to another. Water, a symbol of the emotions, will stagnate if it stops flowing. Equally, feelings need to be allowed to flow if we are to be in equilibrium. This card often represents an inherent conflict that needs to be resolved in a calm and peaceful way. In a difficult relationship, negotiation, compromise, and cooperation are frequently required, as well as the sharing of feelings. Finding a middle path and not going to extremes is the best strategy, and moderation and patience may be needed. The number fourteen is associated with this card, which suggests the need for control, if harmony is to be achieved. Negatively, Temperance indicates the blocking of creative energy and repressed emotions.

Interpretation

This card suggests that you need to adopt a patient, calm, and self-controlled approach to your situation. You are far more likely to achieve a successful outcome if you use diplomacy and moderation in your dealings with others. Communication and the exchange of feelings in a relationship are highlighted, but it is important that you take time to establish how you really feel. You may need to adopt a cautious approach to emotional circumstances. If you remain calm and do not overreact, then you can resolve any difficulties that come your way. Look at both the facts and the feelings, for this will enable you to be both objective and compassionate. Showing temperance in tackling all kinds of different situations will stand you in good stead and will enable you to keep your equilibrium.

Zolar's Astrological Tarot

Successful conclusion to an important undertaking.

MAJOR ARCANA

XIV

KEY 14 — TEMPERANCE

Harmful results due to careless or thought-less decisions.

The Devil

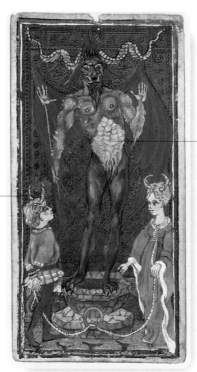

The other face of
Satan is Lucifer, the
"bringer of light,"
reflecting the duality
of this card

The horns, a symbol of
the Devil, connect him
to Satan and all that is
dark and shameful

FRUSTRATIONS ☾ INHIBITIONS ☾ BLOCKS ☾ FEARS
PIERPONT MORGAN VISCONTI-SFORZA TAROT

Many Tarot packs depict the Devil as half-man and half-beast, with
horns and hooves; he generally sits on a throne and has two figures
chained to him. The essence of this card is duality. The other side
of Satan was Lucifer, which means "bringer of light"—a reminder that
light can be found in the midst of darkness. This card describes
the potential that is there to be discovered in the most hidden and
unexpected parts of ourselves, if only we are willing to face up to them
and in the process uncover some of our baser instincts.

Symbolism

The Devil represents the wild and uncivilized aspects of our psyches that we normally tend to repress. We often fear and feel ashamed of these hidden parts of our nature (such as lust, greed, and envy) and choose to disown them. Carl Jung likened these characteristics to what he termed "the shadow" or darker side. The fact that we are so uncomfortable with our base nature means that we frequently project it onto other people, so that we do not have to deal with it ourselves. This tends to wreak havoc in our lives and cause more problems than if we dare openly to acknowledge all of what we are. When we are able to unblock the parts of our psyche that we find unpalatable, a huge amount of positive energy is released. The Devil teaches us to recognize and integrate all aspects of our nature, both the dark and the light. He is a reminder that we are all made up of good and bad. If we can accept our human failings, then we are likely to be more tolerant of others and ourselves and not project blame.

Interpretation

Picking this card suggests that you are likely to meet the darker side of your nature. You might find yourself in an oppressive situation, in which you feel trapped. Rather than projecting your discomfort outward, you may have to face up to something that you find unpleasant about yourself and make it more conscious. Although this is unlikely to be a comfortable experience, it will give you new insights into yourself and will release any repressed negativity that is inhibiting you. Blockages that are hindering your growth are now ready to be removed and you will be able to let go of any self-destructive tendencies. If you wish to develop to your full potential, then sooner or later you need to meet your inner devils and befriend them. This can give rise to real freedom and a more integrated personality.

Marseilles Tarot

The Tower

The Tower has been
struck by lightning
and is on the verge
of disintegrating

The Tower represents
the need to live more
in accordance with
our true self

XVI The Tower

UPHEAVAL (RESTRUCTURING (A NEW ORDER

HERBAL TAROT

This card traditionally shows the only man-made symbol in the Tarot—
a tower that has been hit by lightning and is on the point of collapse.
The Tower represents circumstances and situations in which we find
ourselves that restrict and inhibit our capacity to develop fully. What is
external to us is at variance with our inner truth and needs to be removed
in order for us to grow. The inevitable collapse of the tower is in fact a
blessing in disguise, for it brings with it the realization that the status
quo is imprisoning and no longer supportive.

Symbolism

The Tower indicates that the structures on which we have built our lives need to be torn down, for they no longer support the truth of who we are. This can feel quite alarming, as we may not always be comfortable with abandoning what is familiar, in spite of the fact that we know we are on shaky ground. The Tower heralds a cathartic period, in which anything that has outlived its purpose will simply be eradicated from our lives. We have a chance to clear out the old and build a new structure that supports our beliefs and values. The lightning flash is symbolic of the light that dispels our inner darkness and illuminates a fresh way of being. It is the flash of insight, which prompts us to change our lives and get in line with a deeper truth. In so doing, we free ourselves of the conflict of trying to live according to a false belief system. Sometimes the Tower indicates a radical change of thinking, as we suddenly realize that we can no longer go on in the same way, but need to find a more authentic expression of ourselves. We can feel both liberated and alarmed by this experience, depending on how open to change we are.

Interpretation

The Tower in a reading suggests that you are going through major changes and that things will never be the same again. Your old way of life is collapsing and you have a chance to re-evaluate your lifestyle, rethink what is important to you, and rebuild your life. It is time to be yourself more and dare to live your life more authentically. For example, you may have conformed to the conditioning of your upbringing, but suddenly understand that this no longer reflects who you really are. You need to be prepared to strip away anything that is not truly your own, so that you can live according to your own internal dictates. Even though this can bring turmoil, a new kind of freedom and psychological growth are now possible.

Russian Tarot of St. Petersburg

The Star

The maiden is naked, symbolizing truth, while her youth implies renewed vitality

The water being poured on the land flows into five streams, representing the five senses

HOPE ☾ GOOD FORTUNE ☾ FAITH IN A BETTER FUTURE

ROYAL FEZ MOROCCAN TAROT

A young girl pouring water from two jugs, with stars overhead, is the most common representation of this card. It stands for rebirth, renewal, and hope. From the beginning of time the stars in the heavens have inspired hope, awe, and even reverence. The Star connects us to that part of ourselves that keeps faith, even when life is at its most challenging and there is very little to pin our hopes on. It encourages us to believe in our heart's desire and our most cherished wishes—anything is possible as long as we have hope.

Symbolism

The Star symbolizes a bright and positive outlook and a period in which life begins to come together. It indicates that we can justifiably be optimistic in our expectations and trust in life's bounty. The Star encourages us to open new doors and develop our innate potential. We have a renewed sense of purpose and are able to trust that our hopes and wishes will be fulfilled. The fact that we have a positive expectation helps to attract situations that further our desires and ambitions. "Hope springs eternal" could be the maxim of this card, for deep down within all of us there is a precious sense that our dreams can—and will—come true. When we lose our capacity to trust in the outcome, our inner light dwindles and our lives become lackluster; we become beset with self-doubt and are unable to connect with our capacity to be inspired or guided. The Star represents the light of hope and inspiration, without which we would lose our way. If we are open and receptive, it acts as a guide in times of difficulty and helps us to reach our chosen goal.

Interpretation

When this card appears in a spread, it suggests a renewed sense of purpose. Your energy and your belief in yourself are heightened and you may feel inspired to do something that requires a leap of faith. Life is opening up to you and your sense of hope is what inspires you to follow your dreams. You have a quiet confidence in the future and are unlikely to allow self-doubt to undermine your ability to trust. Hold to your course and know that unexpected blessings can manifest themselves to help you realize your dreams. The Star promises a release from past difficulties. Recent traumas can be overcome and whatever you initiate now will take a positive direction. All you have to do is believe in your own potential.

Universal
Waite Tarot

The Sun

The Sun is an image of rebirth and the light that follows darkness

The two figures represent the two sides of the psyche and symbolize wholeness and integration

ENERGY ☾ OPTIMISM ☾ JOY ☾ CONFIDENCE
SWISS 1JJ TAROT

Traditionally, the Sun is portrayed as a child, or children, in a beautiful garden with the sun overhead. It balances and complements the Moon, but whereas that card represents the dark depths of the unconscious, the Sun symbolizes the illuminated brightness of the conscious mind. It affords clarity of vision and shines a light on darkness and on any uncertainty that we experience. We are able to see our way and know where we are, as well as feeling confident about what the future holds in store for us.

Symbolism

The Sun signifies our capacity to see things clearly and bring order, structure, and coherence to our lives. It represents a source of energy and strength and gives us a feeling of purpose. It is the card of clear perception and clarity of mind and action. The Sun imparts a vision of the future and gives us foresight and the ability to move forward. We intuitively know that we are on course and heading in the right direction. The Sun is associated with Apollo, the Greek god of music and poetry. He also symbolizes the power of the intellect and the masculine function of being able to rationalize our experience. Without this function we would be at the mercy of our fluctuating moods and unable to make sense of where we find ourselves. This card imbues us with optimism, energy, and ambition to pursue our goals and fulfill our desires. It often marks a period of intense creativity and self-expression and a feeling that we are being true to ourselves and developing our unique potential. Not surprisingly, the Sun denotes happiness and joy, as well as a deep sense of fulfillment.

Interpretation

The Sun in a spread indicates contentment and happiness. The darkness is dispelled and you can now see how to resolve any problems. Your thinking is clear and you have the energy and optimism to reach your goals and achieve success. You radiate warmth and well-being and have the self-esteem to give to others, because you have learned to love and accept yourself. You are aware of the more hidden aspects of your nature and have found a way to integrate them in a way that empowers you and gives you a sense of wholeness. Your positive attitude means that you are now able to enjoy life. There may be cause for celebration or you may simply be feeling in peak condition, mentally and physically. You can move forward knowing that you will be successful in whatever you do.

Thoth Tarot

The Moon

The two buildings symbolize the tension of opposites: day and night, light and dark

The crab belongs to both land and sea and reflects the interplay between the conscious and the unconscious mind, between thoughts and feelings

UNCERTAINTY ☾ FLUCTUATION ☾ INTUITION ☾ ILLUSION

MEDIEVAL SCAPINI TAROT

Tarot decks vary in their portrayal of the Moon, but the central theme is invariably a full moon. The moon is connected to the natural waxing and waning of the rhythms of life, to the tides of the ocean, and to the feminine cycle. It also rules the night and is a symbol of the unconscious. Our psyches contain hidden aspects of ourselves, about which we are in the dark. Our inner development requires that we examine our dark side and bring it to light so that we can emerge stronger and more confident as a result.

Symbolism

The Moon is a symbol of our inner
world, which speaks to us through the
language of imagination and dreams.
Something in our psyche is trying to
surface and make itself known to us.
The Moon compels us to understand
the more hidden parts of our nature,
our unconscious impulses and instincts.
These are not always readily accessible
to our conscious minds, but are more
easily expressed through dreams and by
means of creative and artistic pursuits.
Our feelings are often confused and
nebulous when this card appears; we
may even experience hopelessness or
despair. Sometimes we are prone to
delusion or deception, so that we are
unable to see things as they really are.
We feel as if we are groping in the dark
and have very little sense of what the
future holds. We cannot solve our
problems with logic or analysis at this
time. Instead we must rely on our
dreams and intuition to offer us the
insights we need to understand the
more hidden parts of ourselves. Once
these dark corners of our psyches
have been illuminated, we have the
opportunity to incorporate them into
our understanding of ourselves and
become more integrated.

Interpretation

The Moon in a reading denotes that
you are in a period of flux. You may feel
confused or isolated and life can seem
uncertain. Nothing is clear-cut and this
confusing state can leave you feeling
very vulnerable. Fears that you may have
been able to contain in the past may
suddenly break to the surface. For
instance, you may have thought that
you had let go of a past experience or
resolved a particular psychological
pattern, only to have it make its
presence felt again. This does not have
to be negative by any means. If you can
be receptive to messages from the
unconscious, in time you can learn to
integrate the constructive and destructive
energies within your psyche. One positive
way of using this card is to confront
your fears and learn to control them.

**Pierpont Morgan
Visconti-Sforza
Tarot**

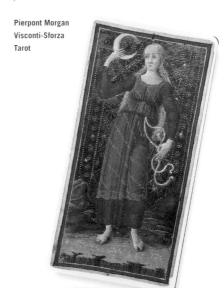

Judgment

The angel is often identified as Archangel Michael, who led the forces of light against darkness in the war of heaven

The naked figures are liberated and ready for a spiritual rebirth and new life

REWARD ☾ COMPLETION ☾ A NEW LEASE OF LIFE
RUSSIAN TAROT OF ST. PETERSBURG

Judgment is often depicted as a figure summoning the dead to rise.
It reflects the fact that, ultimately, all of us have to be accountable for
our actions and face the Day of Reckoning. Judgment marks the
completion of a karmic cycle and indicates that all our deeds have both
positive and negative consequences. Depending on the choices we have
made in our lives, we can either reap the rewards of past efforts and
give ourselves praise for much-deserved successes or we have
some hard lessons to learn.

Symbolism

According to karmic law, each of us is judged after death for our deeds on earth. This card symbolizes the rewards and penalties that we experience, according to the true value of our actions. "As you sow, so shall you reap" is the meaning of this card, and it reflects the need to re-evaluate ourselves and our accomplishments in a frank and honest way. When we reach the end of a chapter, we automatically start a new one, but before we do so, we need to confront the consequences of our past actions and come to terms with the position in which we now find ourselves. Sometimes we can take delight in our achievements to date and have cause to celebrate. At other times we need to come face-to-face with our mistakes or self-betrayals and resolve any conflicts within ourselves. We may not be in total control of our destiny, but our lives are shaped by the decisions we make. Judgment teaches us that we are all in the end responsible for our reality and that the more aware we are of the choices we make, the more responsible we will be for our own individual fate.

Interpretation

This card suggests that it is time to review your life and make sense of how far you have come and what you have achieved. You have the opportunity to wipe the slate clean and make a fresh start by coming to terms with your past. It is time to recognize where you have not lived up to your expectations and make peace with yourself or to reward yourself for past endeavors. Judgment marks a period of consolidation and indicates the importance of taking certain realities on board. A time of harvest is heralded and the promise of a new lease of life. Limiting thoughts and behavior patterns can be transformed, as you are ready to develop an increased sense of awareness and rejoice in the expectation of a better future.

Swiss 1JJ Tarot

The World

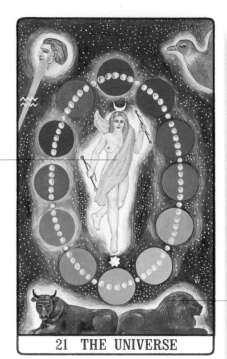

A figure stands within a circle, representing success and completion

The bull, eagle, lion, and man are known as the "guardians of heaven" and represent the four elements and four seasons

21   THE UNIVERSE

SUCCESS ☾ ACHIEVEMENT ☾ REALIZATION OF A GOAL
GOLDEN DAWN TAROT

Like so many other Tarot cards, the World is all about change. It indicates the successful completion of one cycle or stage of life and the beginning of another. This card is connected to the seventeenth-century portrayal of the perfect being as a "crowned hermaphrodite"— a being that is both male and female—and represents integration and completeness. On a deeper level, it suggests harmony with our true nature and a sense of oneness with everything in the universe. Carl Jung defined this as the realization of the Self.

Symbolism

The World signifies a high point in our stage of development and indicates the successful completion of a cycle. It denotes internal and external harmony as a result of being at one with ourselves and finding our place in the scheme of things. Knowing where we belong gives us a sense of peace and well-being. We are more able to flow with life because we know we are part of a something that is bigger than we are. The World reflects our drive for wholeness and independence and our need to function as individuals in our own right—the urge to be ourselves in any given situation, regardless of the circumstances. When we feel complete, we are able to take life in our stride and be guided by what we intuitively know to be right for us. We recognize that everything has a time and a place in our lives, and we accept that the highs and the lows, the light and the dark, are all necessary in order for us to become fully individualized. This card denotes the freedom and exhilaration that we experience when we grow in self-awareness and spiritual understanding.

Interpretation

Choosing this card indicates that you have reached a peak time in your life. Something is coming to fruition and you are able to enjoy a sense of success and achievement. You may be experiencing a deepening spiritual connection and a strong sense of oneness with everything and everyone. You may even feel as if an unseen force that is in tune with your deepest life-purpose is guiding you. This gives you a sense of inner peace and joy and the knowledge that everything is as it should be. Partnerships are also a source of support, because they reflect your inner harmony. You have a sense of being in the right place at the right time and are able to trust that you will be given exactly what you need. You want to acquire greater self-knowledge and expand your understanding of the world.

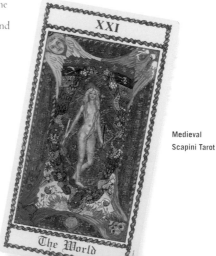

Medieval
Scapini Tarot

THE MAJOR ARCANA AT A GLANCE

Below is a summary of the main symbolism of the cards of the Major Arcana.

CARD	SYMBOLISM
The Fool	Start of a phase, leap of faith, openness to life
The Magician	Guidance, new opportunities, creative initiative
The High Priestess	Esoteric knowledge, intuition, wisdom
The Empress	Abundance, fertility, receptivity
The Emperor	Ambition, authority, worldly success
The Hierophant	Spiritual purpose, self-discovery, inner wisdom
The Lovers	A choice, sacrifice, the testing of a relationship
The Chariot	Conflict, internal struggle, potential for resolution
Justice	Balance, wisdom, fairness
The Hermit	Patience, solitude, reflection
The Wheel of Fortune	Endings and beginnings, a change of circumstances
Strength	Courage, self-confidence, inner resources
The Hanged Man	Sacrifice, transition, spiritual transformation
Death	Endings, rebirth, transformation
Temperance	Cooperation, compromise, moderation
The Devil	Frustration, inhibitions, blocks, fears
The Tower	Upheaval, restructuring, a new order
The Star	Hope, good fortune, faith in a better future
The Sun	Energy, optimism, joy, confidence
The Moon	Uncertainty, fluctuation, intuition, illusion
Judgment	Reward, completion, a new lease of life
The World	Success, achievement, realization of a goal

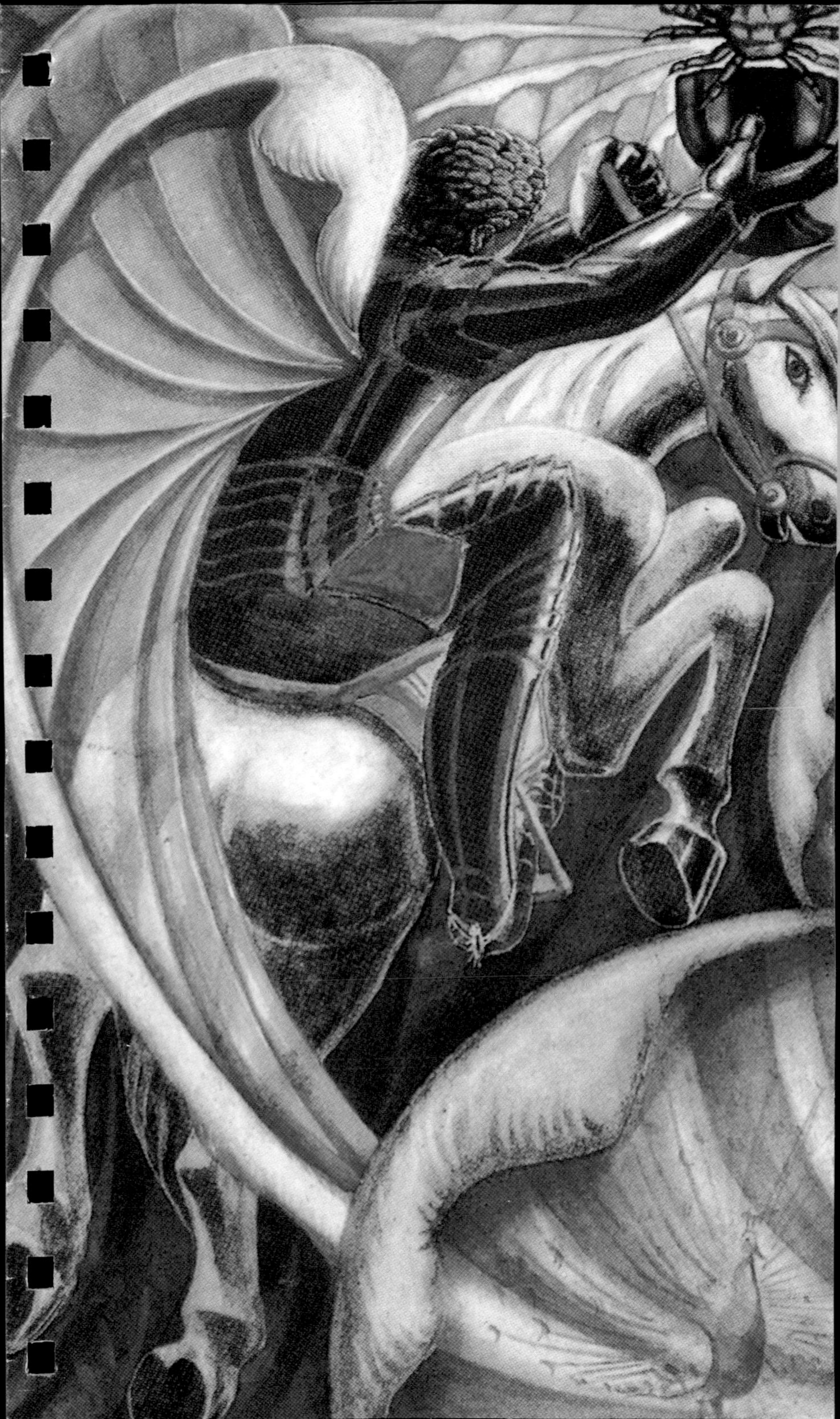

minor arcana

Prince of Disks

The Minor Arcana

The 56 cards of the Minor Arcana are divided into the four suits of Cups, Wands, Pentacles, and Swords. Each suit contains 10 numbered cards (the pip cards) and four court cards (the Page, Knight, Queen, and King). The court cards portray influential people in our lives and aspects of ourselves. The numbered cards reflect our conscious and unconscious motives and indicate future directions we might take. The suit of Cups is connected with feelings and love; Wands with vision and intuition; Pentacles with the material world; Swords with the intellect. The suits also have associations with the four elements.

Ace of Cups

The dove of peace represents spiritual values and the realm of the feelings

The lily indicates the unfolding of our emotional life

EMOTIONAL FULFILLMENT ☾ START OF A RELATIONSHIP
PIERPONT MORGAN VISCONTI-SFORZA TAROT

The suit of Cups is connected with water, the element that rules the feelings and emotions. The Ace is the purest form of emotional energy and will attract love and relationships. The passion and potency of the Ace of Cups represents a surge of emotional energy, often leading to a new relationship or an affair of the heart. Traditionally, this card has been represented by a dove of peace (sometimes depicted carrying a wafer) or by the Holy Grail, which dates back to the stories of King Arthur and symbolizes love, not power, as the ruling force in our lives.

Symbolism

The Ace of Cups is associated with love, marriage, and motherhood. It indicates a time of emotional fulfillment and is an auspicious card for all close relationships. The element of water is associated with the feminine side of our nature and the creative impulse that arises from deep within our soul. We are entering a fruitful period that is rich with possibilities. We are beginning to access our emotional depths and feel a sense of connectedness with others and with ourselves. We feel a sense of peace that comes from being in a happy relationship with another person—we can reap the rewards of being in a loving union and feel truly blessed. Sometimes this card suggests new friendships or the support of colleagues.

Interpretation

When you draw this card, it means that you are starting a fresh chapter in your emotional life. It may mark the beginning of a relationship or a new stage in an existing one. Both love and friendships may have a strong emotional and spiritual quality. The Ace of Cups indicates a time of abundance and that whatever you undertake will be productive. Engagement, marriage, or the birth of a child—and positive beginnings of an emotional nature—are other manifestations. If your creativity has lain dormant or you have been unaware of artistic talents, then you may be about to discover the joy of this side of your nature. You might also be ready to develop your psychic abilities and strengthen your intuition.

Morgan Greer Tarot

Golden Dawn Tarot

ACE OF CUPS

Two of Cups

The lion has wings of the spirit, indicating a balance between spiritual and physical love

A new romance or friendship. Cooperation in partnership affairs.

The two snakes entwined around the staff reflect both the negative and the positive qualities of love

MINOR ARCANA

THE TWO OF CUPS

False promises, instability in emotional matters.

PARTNERS ◖ FRIENDSHIPS ◖ BALANCE OF OPPOSITES

ZOLAR'S ASTROLOGICAL TAROT

The pure energy of the Ace is split in two and a relationship is invoked in this card. The Two of Cups signifies the balance and reconciliation of opposites; quarrels are resolved and harmony is restored. The man and woman often shown exchanging cups are a symbol of the love and emotion that overflowed in the Ace. The difference is that now the energy is both divided and entwined—like the snakes that are curled around the staff—and the interests and needs of two people have to be taken into consideration.

Symbolism

The Two of Cups often describes the early stages of a relationship. If it is a romantic one, this card indicates that there is mutual love and a harmonious balance. It might also indicate potential marriage, an engagement, a love affair, a close supportive friendship, or a business partnership; it can even signify the signing of a contract. The Two of Cups suggests that both romantic and platonic relationships require the spirit of cooperation. If there has been any conflict, it indicates reconciliation so that a new phase can begin. If we are thinking of taking a partner, this card indicates that we are making the right choice. A balance between spiritual and physical love is one of the highest manifestations of the Two of Cups.

Interpretation

Choosing the Two of Cups indicates that you are about to experience the joy of being in a relationship. Whether you are embarking on a love affair or a business partnership, this card suggests that you will be able to rely on this person and have complete trust in them, for the Two of Cups describes a relationship of equals. If you have recently fallen out with someone, this card is telling you that reconciliation is possible because you are willing to forgive and forget and renew the relationship on a fresh footing. The Two of Cups denotes a time of healing, in which peace can be restored after a period of disharmony. You are able to share feelings and ideas with your partner and create a strong bond.

Herbal Tarot

Swiss 1JJ Tarot

Uva Ursi

Two of Cups

Three of Cups

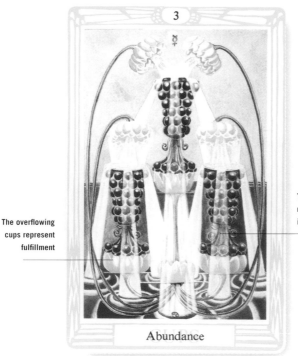

The overflowing cups represent fulfillment

This is one of the most joyous cards in the Tarot

Abundance

REJOICING ☾ CELEBRATION ☾ JOY
THOTH TAROT

The number three here stands for the completion of the first stage of a process. A foundation has been laid in the Ace of Cups that bears fruit in the Two. With the Three of Cups there is a sense of having achieved something of great emotional value, and it indicates a time of festivity. This card usually illustrates overflowing cups or a joyous occasion: the Universal Waite Tarot shows three women dancing in happy celebration and raising their cups in the air. However, as with all the threes, there is still much to do before the ultimate fulfillment of this suit is reached.

Symbolism

The Three of Cups is a card of great happiness. The first flush of a relationship is behind us and we are now ready to make a commitment to the future. This marks a time of rejoicing, but the Three of Cups does not describe the final outcome of the relationship and reminds us that there is still a long way to go before we can feel that we are firmly established as a couple. This is a healing card: spiritually, emotionally, and physically. It affirms our faith in the future and supports our belief that everything will turn out for the best. Any kind of joyous event is indicated from a wedding to the birth of a child (although sometimes "birth" relates to a spiritual or creative level). We are ready to grow and express ourselves in new ways with this card, and we may be developing psychically or embarking on an artistic project that is deeply satisfying to us.

Interpretation

When you select the Three of Cups, you are ready to experience great emotional happiness. Whatever you are celebrating, you are reaping the rewards of your earlier endeavors. You have a deep sense of well-being and can bask in the knowledge that you are loved and valued by others. You delight in the company of loved ones and have a great sense of optimism about the future. This card may also indicate recovery from illness or an unhappy situation, and suggests that you will soon experience a change of fortunes for the better.

**Medieval
Scapini Tarot**

**Universal
Waite Tarot**

Four of Cups

Taking responsibility for the status quo will bring about change

The man refusing the cups being handed to him is too jaded to appreciate what he is being offered

Four of Cups

DISCONTENT ☾ DISSATISFACTION ☾ BOREDOM
RUSSIAN TAROT OF ST. PETERSBURG

The solid nature of number four and the unpredictability of our emotions make for an uncomfortable mix. This is the card of divine discontent and describes a situation in which, for various reasons, there is an inability to appreciate what we have. A man is frequently shown on this card looking too apathetic to accept the opportunity that is being offered to him, in the form of a fourth cup. Alternatively, four cups overflowing with good things may be depicted, but our inherent dissatisfaction with life prevents us from appreciating them.

Symbolism

The Four of Cups depicts a state of boredom or apathy, in which we are too preoccupied to appreciate the good things that surround us. Opportunities are there for the taking, but our inertia prevents us from seeing them. We may feel as if we are stuck in a rut but unable to muster the energy to break free. This card does not necessarily mean that our circumstances warrant such dissatisfaction. We may have everything we need, but somehow take our good fortune for granted. We are in danger of getting into a negative emotional pattern in which we fail to recognize the qualities of those around us. The grass may appear greener on the other side, or we may long for something— or someone—that is unavailable.

Interpretation

When this card appears in a spread, you are being asked to adopt a fresh approach to life and to re-evaluate your position. You have become disenchanted with the status quo, in spite of the fact that you have a lot to be grateful for. Life has become dull and you feel the need to introduce some variety. You may be feeling below par or out of sorts, particularly where relationships are concerned; you may even feel resentful, unloved, or be nursing a grudge. This period may seem like an anticlimax after an emotional high point. The message of the Four of Cups is that there is a chance for emotional growth, but you need to be willing to move forward and not remain entrenched in an outworn pattern of thinking.

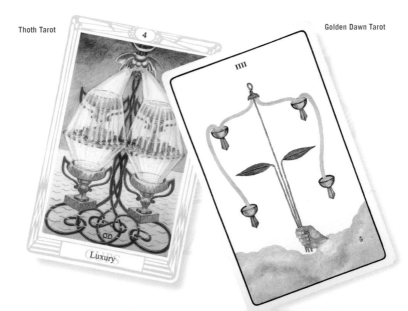

Thoth Tarot

Golden Dawn Tarot

Luxury

Five of Cups

V

The black cloak symbolizes mourning

The upright cups suggest that all is not lost

SORROW ☾ MELANCHOLY ☾ DISAPPOINTMENT IN LOVE
MORGAN GREER TAROT

The number five is associated with flux and uncertainty. The overturned cups often depicted on this card symbolize a disappointment, particularly in a relationship, bringing much sadness—over which a sorrowful figure shrouded in a black cloak is sometimes shown weeping. But what has been lost is not necessarily irretrievable, for one or two cups usually remain upright, suggesting that painful emotional experiences can lead to a turn of the tide, if we are willing to acknowledge that there is still something left to build on.

Symbolism

In this card a change in relationships takes place. There is a need to let go of something and this brings with it regret. However, the cups that remain standing indicate that there is still something positive on which to build. We need to focus on what is redeemable and take on board the fact that, for the time being, we have reached an impasse. We have an opportunity to address our emotional values and review our relationship to others. We might be going through an emotionally painful time, but this may be necessary in order to make some fundamental changes. It may be difficult to understand what is being required of us, but the Five of Cups indicates that it is possible to salvage something and this gives us hope for the future.

Interpretation

When you pick the Five of Cups, you may be feeling a deep sense of loss. You may think that you have made a poor or wrong choice. An argument may have led to a separation and suddenly everything looks bleak. A relationship has gone wrong and you may have no choice but to let go. Although this card marks a period of disappointment, it also indicates that there are still hopeful possibilities for the future. Something of value remains and it is up to you to build on what is intact. It is important not to immerse yourself in self-pity; otherwise you will fail to act on the positive message of this card. Look back with regret if you have to—but remember that you still have everything to hope for.

Marseilles Tarot

Pierpont Morgan Visconti-Sforza Tarot

Six of Cups

A young man offers a goblet of flowers to a young girl

Five goblets of colorful blooms stand nearby, representing fruitfulness

PAST EFFORTS BEAR FRUIT IN THE PRESENT
ROYAL FEZ MOROCCAN TAROT

The Six of Cups indicates a move away from a stressful situation and the end of an anxious phase. It is now possible to overcome any obstacles and pass into a more relaxed state of mind, although it will take time for everything to be fully resolved. Emotionally, a new phase is beginning, perhaps with a resurgence of youthful desires, as represented in many decks by a young man offering fruit or flowers to a girl. Sometimes an older child is depicted helping a younger one, and the Six of Cups is often viewed as signifying a happy childhood.

Symbolism

The Six of Cups symbolizes the beginning of a new cycle, as long as we are able to accept the past and the way in which events have transpired. This is the card of nostalgia and, when we choose it, we may have a tendency to dwell on the past or to romanticize the experiences we have had. Although the future beckons and we have every opportunity to move on, we may still be plagued by memories that we have not been able to let go of. The Six of Cups reminds us that, however much we wish to idealize the past, we are in danger of jeopardizing our future if we do so and must reconcile ourselves with what has happened. Time is needed to mull over what has gone before so that a course of action can be decided upon.

Interpretation

Choosing the Six of Cups suggests that you may be living too much in the past and not focusing enough on what is yet to come. You may be reminiscing about time gone by, or feeling sad about people who once meant a lot to you, but who are now no longer in your life. Or you might need to take stock of the past in order to resolve any difficulties that may be preventing you from moving forward. A lover or an old friend might reappear in your life, or a love affair that you thought had died might suddenly be revived. Alternatively, you might reap the rewards of the hard work that you have done. The future awaits you—and, far from having diminished you, your experiences have made you all the stronger.

A new beginning. A radical change from old time associations and environments.

THE SIX OF CUPS

6 ♥

MINOR ARCANA

9 ♥

A call for the payment of an old debt.

Zolar's Astrological Tarot

Watermelon

Six of Cups

Herbal Tarot

Seven of Cups

The cups floating on clouds represent fantasies and dreams

The lower row of cups represents power and greed

MAKING A REALISTIC CHOICE ❈ CREATIVE POTENTIAL
UNIVERSAL WAITE TAROT

The number seven relates to dreams, fantasies, and imaginative ideas. The Seven of Cups challenges our aspirations and represents the need to be realistic about the choices that are made, for not everything is worth pursuing. Seven cups either dripping with excess or floating on clouds and revealing strange and wonderful fantasies are usually shown—in the Universal Waite Tarot one of these images is even portrayed as a "castle in the air." The upper row symbolizes a deeper connection with the unconscious, while the lower row represents ambition and greed.

Symbolism

The Seven of Cups describes the need to choose between various options and determine which are grounded in reality and which are simply castles in the air. All of them are appealing in some way, but not everything will live up to its promise. This can be a confusing time when we are being pulled in different directions. There is a danger that we will spend our time daydreaming instead of making our fantasies real. We need to act, for once we have commiteed ourselves, our energy will no longer be dissipated by indecision. The Seven of Cups indicates an abundance of imaginative gifts that should not be wasted. We need to find ways to channel our creativity into worthwhile activities so that our talents are given expression.

Interpretation

Drawing this card indicates that you have decisions to make regarding an emotional situation. Many options are open to you, but you need to think them through carefully in order to make an informed choice. Your intuition senses all kinds of potential, but these dreams must be made real and concrete, or they will forever remain in the realms of fantasy. Your imagination is working overtime and you may be reluctant to give up all your daydreams. However, the Seven of Cups reminds you that nothing will come of your hopes unless you act decisively and work hard to bring them to fruition. You may be challenged to find ways of expressing your artistic talents, for there is much opportunity for fulfillment in this area.

Swiss 1JJ Tarot

Thoth Tarot

Debauch

Eight of Cups

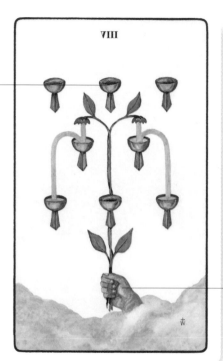

VIII

The eight cups symbolize resignation to our situation and the need to move on

Although the cups are full, the emotional situation may have been outgrown

LETTING GO ☾ ABANDONING HOPE
GOLDEN DAWN TAROT

Eight is the number of death and rebirth. The Eight of Cups suggests

leaving behind an emotional situation that has outlived its usefulness.

There is an opportunity to start something new, as long as the process of

letting go is unconditional. In the Morgan Greer Tarot, the figure of a

cloaked man is shown walking toward a barren mountain. He has turned

his back on eight standing cups, knowing that it is time to move on. The

Moon is depicted in both its full and waning quarters, signifying that

something has come to an end.

Symbolism

With the Eight of Cups we are being asked to abandon what is familiar and to face our fears of the unknown. We may have given our all to an emotional situation, only to discover that it has not lived up to our hopes. Our expectations are dashed and we have no choice but to move on. The sense of disillusionment at the end of a relationship can be extremely painful, especially if we have invested all of our aspirations in it. We are forced to recognize that something is not working and that we must leave it behind, in the hope that we will find something more meaningful. This card implies a sense of resignation, as well as acceptance that we now need to start a fresh chapter. No matter how hard it is to face up to our circumstances, the choice to end something is nevertheless voluntary. We have ceased to grow and the only answer to this feeling of stasis is to walk away.

Interpretation

The end of one situation and the beginning of something new is the message of this card. An emotional situation has outlived its purpose and you have no alternative but to say goodbye. The disappointment may be hard to bear; you may be feeling bereft and emotionally insecure and in need of time to heal. It is important to take care of yourself now and to pay attention to your feelings. Ultimately, however, the changes will prove beneficial, even though you still have upheavals to face and adjustments to make.

Morgan Greer Tarot

VIII

Pierpont Morgan Visconti-Sforza Tarot

Nine of Cups

Nine cups raised on pillars signify pleasure and contentment

The main figure is surrounded by lush, abundant foliage

Nine of Cups

EMOTIONAL FULFILLMENT ☾ TRUE CONTENTMENT
HERBAL TAROT

The Nine of Cups is known as the "wish card" of the Minor Arcana.
True happiness in love is indicated and the fulfillment of heartfelt
desires. An emotional commitment of some kind that brings joy is its
message. In many decks, the principal figure's happy expression bears
testimony to the fact that this card marks a high point of emotional
fulfillment and the realization of a dream come true; in other decks, such
as the Marseilles Tarot, the nine cups may be overflowing with happiness
that pours forth from lotus flowers.

Symbolism

The Nine of Cups suggests that a desire of great importance is coming true. Our hopes of finding true love are finally realized and we can rejoice in the ecstasy of mutual affection. Sensual pleasure and deep emotional, physical, and material satisfaction are symbolized by this card. We are able to delight in our senses and enjoy the giving and receiving of pleasure. An inner as well as an outer union takes place, because not only are we making an emotional commitment to someone, but a commitment to our own true values. The Nine of Cups represents the rewards we receive when we have made a pledge to our highest emotional aspirations. The trials and tribulations that have led us to this point now yield a joyous relationship.

Interpretation

If you select the Nine of Cups, you are ready to enjoy happiness and prosperity in abundance. This is the card of emotional, physical, and material well-being and suggests a time of personal contentment. You are feeling confident about the goals that you have reached. A marriage is possible, or you may be starting a sensuous love affair; you may be about to secure a business deal or finalize a project of great value to you. Whatever your circumstances, you want to share your contentment with others. Love, friendship, and the company of close ones are all to be enjoyed. You feel justifiably pleased with yourself and your achievements, and those around you want to show how much they care for you by sharing your new-found joy.

Marseilles Tarot

Russian Tarot of St. Petersburg

Nine of Cups

Ten of Cups

The rainbow
is a representation of
hope and promise

The entwined arms are
a symbol of the couple's
emotional security

HARMONY IN RELATIONSHIPS ☾ COOPERATION
MORGAN GREER TAROT

The number ten means that something has reached a state of perfection
and is now complete. This card indicates a sense of permanence in the
emotional realms and the culmination of everything we could wish for.
It reflects a sense of emotional harmony, peace, and genuine happiness.
A happy and harmonious family scene is often featured on this card,
with an embracing couple standing before a rainbow. Dancing children
beside them may be holding hands, indicating cooperation and the
aspirations of future generations.

Symbolism

The Ten of Cups symbolizes joy in a marriage, relationship, friendship, or partnership. Success is assured and we can rest secure in the knowledge that we have reached our personal goals. This card indicates lasting happiness, which has been achieved through our own efforts. Although we still need to work at our relationships in order for them to grow, the Ten of Cups suggests that we have found what we are looking for. Nothing can permanently threaten our harmony. This card marks the summation of the potential of the suit of Cups and indicates the pinnacle of what can be achieved in terms of love and happiness. The Ten of Cups also describes a state of spiritual harmony that comes from valuing ourselves for what we are.

Interpretation

When the Ten of Cups appears in a spread, it means that a cherished wish will be granted. You have a feeling of emotional security and permanence that gives rise to a deep sense of well-being. Family life is a source of much happiness, and the birth of a child may be indicated. You are able to extend the love and passion of your union to your children. This card describes a happy home and good relationships with others. You are able to give yourself freely to those around you. You have gained a feeling of peace and there is a strong sense that everything in your life is working out for the best. On the emotional front, you can expect the most positive of outcomes. All of your needs in this respect are provided for.

Royal Fez Moroccan Tarot

Golden Dawn Tarot

Page of Cups

The fish is a symbol of creative imagination

The light pink and blue colors reflect the softness and gentleness of the suit of Cups

Princess of Cups

FRESH BEGINNINGS ☾ SELF-LOVE ☾ A NEW RELATIONSHIP

THOTH TAROT

All the Pages are bearers of news, and the Page of Cups brings news of a birth—either that of a child or the birth of a fresh attitude. There is a sense of renewal on an emotional level after a painful experience. The Page of Cups is frequently shown carrying a large goblet of water with a fish in it, the symbol of creative imagination. As the Page gazes at the cup, the fish emerges from it, indicating the birth of creative imagination and a new life. In the Thoth Tarot, the Page is known as the Princess and emerges in a swirl of energy.

Symbolism

The Pages symbolize potential, and the Page of Cups represents possibilities in the emotional realm. He brings the message of self-love, especially if we have been hurt, and indicates that we are beginning to trust again, although we need time to allow our feelings to develop. Perhaps a new relationship or the birth of a child acts as a catalyst. If the Page of Cups relates to a person in our lives, then he or she is likely to be open-hearted, warm, and charming. The Page may also describe a sensitive or artistic young person who is loving, thoughtful, reflective, and altruistic. Alternatively, these qualities may be in embryonic form within us and ready to manifest. As with all the Pages, these qualities need careful nurturing.

Interpretation

When the Page of Cups shows in your reading, it indicates that you are ready to get in touch with your feelings— something opens you up again to the inner world of your emotions. Tender care is needed to bring this situation to fruition because everything is still fragile at this stage. You may be about to discover latent skills and talents, which could be of an artistic or psychic nature. You are now more in tune with your inner world and may feel inspired to be more creative. The Page of Cups describes a need for reflection and contemplation. You may decide to begin studying or take up a new interest or hobby that both fascinates and inspires you and brings you into contact with the world of the unconscious.

Universal
Waite Tarot

Swiss 1JJ
Tarot

PAGE of CUPS

PAGE of CUPS

Knight of Cups

The golden chalice symbolizes spiritual aspirations

The Knight of Cups looks out into the distance

KNIGHT OF CUPS

A PROPOSAL ☾ LOVE ☾ ROMANCE

MARSEILLES TAROT

The Knight of Cups heralds a proposal of some kind, which may or
may not be grounded in reality. The practical implications need to be
considered carefully before a commitment is made. The handsome,
dashing figure of the Knight usually carries a golden chalice and wears
a winged helmet—both of which represent spiritual aspirations.
He is ready to fight for an ideal or a sentiment that is important to him,
and may be likened to the Knights of the Holy Grail and their quest
for truth, beauty, and love.

Symbolism

All of the Knights signify a period of transition; in the case of the Knight of Cups, this relates to the realm of feelings. If this card relates to a person, then he is likely to be idealistic, artistic, sensitive, and imaginative; he may be extremely seductive and embody the qualities of the romantic lover. Alternatively, we may now be ready for love and this in turn will attract a relationship to us. We may receive a proposal of marriage or be swept off our feet. The Knight of Cups may also represent the cultivation of our own idealism, romanticism, and creativity. We may develop an interest in the arts or be ready to embark on a spiritual search. The Knight of Cups can help us to reach greater depths in our psyche.

Interpretation

When you draw the Knight of Cups, it suggests new possibilities with regard to personal relationships, love, and marriage. You may meet someone who exemplifies the attributes of this card and who has an intoxicating effect on you. The Knight of Cups indicates that there are changes on the horizon that encompass the world of feelings, as well as creative and artistic pursuits. You feel ready to embark on a new quest: you may be in search of an ideal that proves elusive, but still holds true for you. You have a strong desire to express your love of beauty and truth—whether through relationships or in a creative form. If you meet someone who encapsulates the Knight's qualities, it may signify that these qualities are ready to manifest in you.

Morgan Greer Tarot

Medieval Scapini Tarot

Queen of Cups

The Queen of Cups
looks intently at the
chalice, symbol of
her power

Peace and serenity
are evident on the
Queen's face

QUEEN OF CUPS

INTUITION ❲ NURTURING ❲ RECEPTIVITY
GOLDEN DAWN TAROT

The Queens may represent either significant women in our lives or
qualities that are of relevance within us at the time of a reading. The
Queen of Cups is highly intuitive by nature and is quite at home in her
inner world. She is traditionally shown seated on an ornate throne at the
edge of the shore. This suggests that she is both immersed in life and at
the same time remains open to the forces of the unconscious and to her
deeper feelings. Because water is the most feminine of the elements and
is associated with this suit, this is a very powerful card.

Symbolism

The Queen of Cups is a very passionate woman, who is fully in touch with her feelings. She is calm and contained and has a highly developed capacity for introspection. Her sensitivity and gentleness make her loved and adored. The fact that she has hidden depths and does not reveal all of herself gives her an air of mystery and makes her beguiling. To a large extent she lives in the world of fantasy—she may even have a mystical quality about her. The Queen is both intuitive and artistic and can use her creative skills in a number of ways. She represents receptivity to the needs of others, and draws people to her who are ready to connect more deeply to their inner world. She is also capable of nurturing others.

Interpretation

A readiness to express your innermost feelings to the world is the message of the Queen of Cups. Someone who embodies her qualities may play a significant role in your life, or you may be ready to embrace these attributes for yourself. You may be about to start a project that gives your creative or artistic skills greater expression, or to embark on a relationship that is warm, loving, and sensual. This card suggests that you are tuned into the promptings of your unconscious mind and the inspiration that springs from within. Your foresight and maturity will help you to make choices that are beneficial to you. Your ability to know how you are feeling acts as a strong harmonious influence that others find endearing.

Russian Tarot of St. Petersburg

Queen of Cups

Royal Fez Moroccan Tarot

King of Cups

The fish around the
King's neck symbolizes
creative imagination

The turbulent seas are
indicative of the ebb
and flow of this suit

KING of CUPS.

KINDNESS ☾ FRIENDLINESS ☾ EMPATHY
UNIVERSAL WAITE TAROT

The Kings in the Minor Arcana may represent important men in
our lives or an aspect of us that is emerging, but which needs to
be harnessed. The King of Cups is considerate and friendly, but
undemonstrative. A fish, symbol of spirituality and creative imagination,
normally leaps out of the sea in the distance or is worn as an emblem
around the King's neck. His feet do not touch the water, suggesting that
he has mastery over his emotions, perhaps because he does not really
connect with his element.

Symbolism

The King of Cups is often seen in the role of adviser on emotional matters and on the spiritual well-being of others. He may be a doctor, a counsellor, or a healer. He commands great respect and has a deep understanding of the human condition. But although he is honest and caring and has a wonderful capacity to empathize with others, he remains detached. He is reliable and well-meaning and offers us good advice; he genuinely wants to give of his time and be supportive to others, but finds it difficult to express his feelings. He represents a paradox inasmuch as he wants to engage in a deep, intimate relationship but at the same time he is frightened by such powerful desires. He may be embarrassed about his emotions and has learned to master them, but even though this is beneficial for him professionally, it gives rise to difficulties in personal relationships.

Interpretation

Choosing the King of Cups indicates that it is time to get in touch with your own feelings. You have the chance to become more open, perhaps with the help of a therapist, teacher, or someone in the caring professions who helps you access your inner world; or you may meet someone who pays lip service to this. More positively, the King of Cups signifies someone who is able to channel their intuitive and creative skills into their work, for the benefit of others. The potential to become more involved with life is the gift of the King of Cups.

Swiss 1JJ Tarot

Herbal Tarot

KING of CUPS

Saw Palmetto

King of Cups

Ace of Wands

The budding wand
represents new ideas

The strong hand holding
the wand signifies the
power of this suit

A SURGE OF ENERGY ☾ ENTHUSIASM
SWISS 1JJ TAROT

The suit of Wands (or Clubs or Rods, as it is sometimes known) represents action, initiative, movement, enterprise, energy, and growth. It is associated with the element of fire, which in psychological terms is called intuition. This in turn is linked to the world of creative visualization, imagination, and fantasy. The Ace of Wands is the creative life force in its purest form. It embodies the full power, vision, and motivation of the suit and suggests that fresh ideas and impulses are breaking through and are ready to manifest themselves.

Symbolism

As the first card, the Ace represents the driving force and raw potential of the suit of Wands. This card indicates a powerful surge of enthusiasm. A wonderfully new phase is heralded and there is an abundance of innovative ideas. Foundations can be laid for creative ventures, but the vision embodied in this card needs to be backed up by a strong commitment to the new goal. Inspiration, optimism, and renewed energy are required to dream up fresh projects. The suit of Wands often indicates worldly aspirations in terms of career, and this card may symbolize a business venture with the potential to succeed. All that is needed is faith in our ability to conjure up a vision and manifest it in the world.

Interpretation

Choosing this card indicates that you are full of creative ideas and feeling a strong impulse to put them into action. Your dream will prove challenging, but it will be worth the effort. You are on the threshold of a new beginning— perhaps embarking in a fresh direction in your life or starting a new enterprise. You have a strong desire to channel your energies into something creative. You may experience a sudden breakthrough that enables you to envisage a goal that is both daunting and exciting. Life is flowing fast and you are eager to get out into the world. However, remember the saying, "Fools rush in where angels fear to tread"—do not be in too much of a rush, for impulsive decisions could undermine your success.

Morgan Greer Tarot

ACE OF RODS

Medieval
Scapini Tarot

Two of Wands

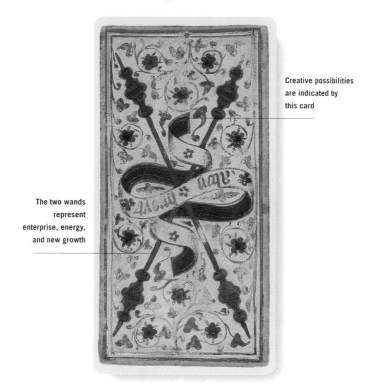

Creative possibilities are indicated by this card

The two wands represent enterprise, energy, and new growth

A GOAL OR PROJECT ☾ FORMULATING A NEW IDEA

PIERPONT MORGAN VISCONTI-SFORZA TAROT

The Two of Wands suggests that the formulation of a new project still remains possible. The ideas that were envisioned with the Ace are beginning to take root, but they still have a long way to go before their potential can manifest itself fully. In many decks a man stands on a castle wall, holding a wand in his left hand (symbol of what he has achieved) and a globe in his right hand (signifying future possibilities). He appears to be deciding on his next move and the sprouting leaves on the wands point to creative potential as yet unfulfilled.

Symbolism

The Two of Wands implies that we are now ready to do something with the inspiration represented by the Ace of Wands. It indicates a time of transition and suggests that success, progress, and growth are all possible. There is a strong feeling of change and restlessness that encourages us to move forward. The Two of Wands suggests that our endeavors will be rewarded, provided we can overcome the obstacles in our path. We have far to travel, but our ideas are established firmly enough for us to take the next step. The powerful energy of the Ace, coupled with the strong single-mindedness of Wands, indicates that we have got what it takes to attain our ambition. We are willing to put ourselves to the test to realize our potential. However, because of the duality of the number two, we may be at odds with ourselves, or there may be some inner conflict to resolve.

Interpretation

New opportunities are being offered to you when you draw this card. It is time to take stock of your situation and plan ahead. You may need to re-evaluate your career and decide where you should go from here, or the opportunity of a business partnership or a joint venture could present itself. The Two of Wands suggests that your circumstances look set to improve, but you need to give yourself time to think things through. Even though you may feel some anxiety, this card implies that you have the courage to move forward.

Royal Fez Moroccan Tarot

Thoth Tarot

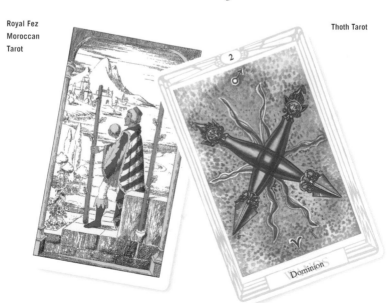

Dominion

Three of Wands

The resting figure suggests the initial completion of a project

The figures scaling the obstacle suggest the hurdles that have yet to be overcome

COMPLETION OF THE FIRST STAGE ☾ OPTIMISM
MEDIEVAL SCAPINI TAROT

The inspirational energy of the Ace of Wands and the setting-in-motion of the Two is fulfilled in the Three of Wands (or Clubs). This card marks the initial completion of whatever was started with the Ace, although it also suggests there is much work to do—as represented by the climbers in the Medieval Scapini Tarot. In the Herbal Tarot, a man is seen looking out over a landscape that is barren, except for a large sprouting saffron in the foreground, which implies that there are opportunities for development and that something has already started to grow.

Symbolism

The Three of Wands symbolizes new possibilities. Although we may have realized a dream, we become aware that there is even farther to travel. Exciting new opportunities, of which we may not previously have been aware, are now opening up and we are ready to continue what was set in motion with the Ace. A fresh momentum is being generated and we feel motivated to launch ourselves into the task at hand. This card represents the strength and determination that are needed to persevere with our goals. It indicates that we must remain focused. The Three of Wands is an excellent indication of a favorable outcome and suggests that the time is ripe to promote ourselves and allow our talents to shine.

Interpretation

If this card appears in a spread, it indicates that you are full of creative ideas. You may be embarking on a fresh career or way of life and you feel optimistic about the future, although you may need to bide your time temporarily to see how your ideas develop. This is not a time to rest on your laurels, however, as there is still much to do. No matter how far you have come, the Three of Wands indicates that there is much more to accomplish. This is an excellent moment to communicate your ideas to others. The Three of Wands suggests movement and attests to the fact that you are ready for the next challenge. You feel satisfied with what you have achieved so far and confident and excited about the path ahead.

Russian Tarot of St. Petersburg

Herbal
Tarot

Three of Wands

Three of Clubs

Four of Wands

The garland represents happiness and celebration

The castle is a symbol of success

JOY ☾ CELEBRATION AFTER HARD WORK
MORGAN GREER TAROT

The Four of Wands signifies a time of well-deserved celebration.
It suggests enjoyment and relaxation, as well as creative achievement.
It sometimes indicates a holiday or a rest at the end of exams or a period
of hard work. After this, there will be even more incentive to continue
the quest. In Zolar's Astrological Tarot a jubilant couple wave garlands
above their heads in a spirit of festivity, while four wands in the
foreground are also decorated with ribbons, fruit, and flowers. A bridge
over a moat leading to a castle signifies the goal that has been achieved.

Symbolism

The Four of Wands symbolizes the well-earned break that we all need after our labors. It denotes a period of tranquility in which we can justifiably take pride in our accomplishments. Four is the number of stability and, when this combines with the energy of the suit of Wands, it results in a very buoyant and productive card. Both Wands and fire embrace freedom and expansion, but in this card there is a solid foundation on which to build for the future. Four is known as the number of wholeness and this card testifies to the well-being that we feel. However, there is also a sense that life has much more to offer.. This card indicates that there is plenty of scope to manifest our inner growth in a creative way.

Interpretation

Drawing the Four of Wands suggests that you are in the full flow of life and ready to express your creativity and innate talents. There is a feeling of joy and stability in your life and you are able to relax and take it easy for a while. You have something to celebrate and are feeling a strong sense of achievement. There is a calm, stable, and harmonious atmosphere around you, which helps you to unwind and let go of any stresses and strains you have been carrying. You have successfully completed a task and, in spite of the fact that there is much hard work ahead, you feel secure in the knowledge that you have done what you set out to do. This card suggests that you have reached a plateau and that the rest will prepare you for the climb ahead.

Marseilles Tarot

Zolar's Astrological Tarot

Five of Wands

The battle with the wands suggests a time of conflict ahead

The fact that the figures do not really hurt each other implies that competition is healthy

STRUGGLES (IRRITATION (COMPETITION
UNIVERSAL WAITE TAROT

The Five of Wands denotes a period of uncertainty. Nothing goes according to plan and everything feels like an uphill struggle. Certain obstacles need to be overcome in order to realize a goal that is within sight. Courage and patience will be required. Most decks feature five men locked in combat in some way, each brandishing a wand. There is a conflict of interests and each figure is being challenged to compete against the others in order to test their skills and see how competent they are in the face of opposition.

Symbolism

This card symbolizes the challenges that we meet when we attempt to manifest our ideas in the material world. The inspired vision of the suit of Wands comes face-to-face with the brick wall of reality. Our ability to handle difficult situations is tested as we are forced to compete with others and rely on our wits. We may need to draw on all our resources to be effective and to deal with challenges or adversity. There is a strong desire to resolve a situation by squaring up to others and not backing down. Although this card indicates that some kind of trouble is unavoidable, it suggests that we have sufficient energy to deal with it effectively. This will equip us to contend with the confrontations implicit in this card.

Interpretation

The Five of Wands in a spread indicates a trying time ahead, during which you have to deal with all sorts of irritations. You may be locked in a power struggle or you may be ambivalent in your opinions, resulting in arguments and frustrations. There is a strong sense of challenge about this card. Delays or misunderstandings hold up your ability to move forward and it may seem that nothing is going right. The problems you are facing are time-consuming and you may be required to make a compromise, but it is important to keep your goals in sight and not allow yourself to lose heart. Although the challenges you face are not especially serious or long-term, you still have to find a way of surmounting them.

Morgan Greer Tarot

Golden Dawn Tarot

Six of Wands

Two of the wands bear the wings of Victory

The six wands are crossed to form the shape of an "X"

Victory

SUCCESS ❨ VICTORY ❨ ACCOMPLISHMENT
THOTH TAROT

This is a card of achievement in the world and of well-deserved success. The commitment that was needed to bring something to completion is being rewarded and there is a sense of accomplishment. Six is the number of harmony and is generally associated with recognition for effort and hard work. It is sometimes depicted as a man riding a horse and wearing a laurel wreath or, more generally, as six wands interwoven to form an "X" shape (called "Victory" in the Thoth Tarot). It reflects both contentment with the present and a sense of striving in the future.

Symbolism

The Six of Wands indicates a peak of achievement: a moment of triumph when we can reap the rewards of our dedicated efforts. This card marks the end of one cycle and reminds us that a new phase is about to begin. Its inherent paradox is that it represents recognition of what we have gained so far and an understanding that there is still much to do. In other words, it does not guarantee success in the long term, but emphasizes the successes that we have managed to achieve to date. The Six of Wands marks an exciting time when we can enjoy the acknowledgment of others. Everything that we have done in the past to help us reach this point is now acclaimed. This in turn gives us a certain self-confidence, which may inspire others to achieve similar heights. The message of this card is enjoy this time of victory but to keep focused on the goals that have yet to be reached.

Interpretation

Selecting this card suggests that you can enjoy a period of success: you may receive promotion or your job prospects may look positive; you may gain a qualification or pass some exams. The Six of Wands often indicates public acclaim and honor. There is a promise of fulfillment. You are feeling optimistic and can justifiably rest on your laurels for a bit, knowing that you deserve the accolades that are coming your way. However, you also know that you cannot stay where you are forever and will soon need to move toward new challenges.

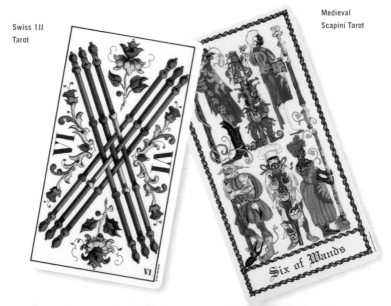

Swiss 1JJ
Tarot

Medieval
Scapini Tarot

Six of Wands

Seven of Wands

The bird symbolizes the possibility of a more peaceful outcome

The young man brandishing a wand represents courage in adversity

Seven of Clubs

COMPETITION (COURAGE (DETERMINATION

RUSSIAN TAROT OF ST. PETERSBURG

The Seven of Wands presents a challenge to fight one's corner and defend one's beliefs. The peak moment experienced with the Six of Wands may be under threat and it is necessary to learn to hold onto what was gained. Six wands are often shown rising up to attack a young man who, brandishing a seventh wand, is courageously fighting back. In the Royal Fez Moroccan Tarot he needs to look ahead and be on his guard, because he is dangerously near the edge of a precipice and could easily fall into it unless he takes care.

Symbolism

The Seven of Wands represents a time when we have to work extremely hard—and sometimes even fight for what we have. After gaining much ground with the Six, we are now confronted with the reality of what will happen if we do not hold onto it, and with finding a way of both defending and improving our current position. We may feel embattled, but this card suggests that we have the fortitude to fend off the competition and secure our place in the scheme of things. The Seven of Wands is a spur to growth, because healthy competition encourages us to achieve our personal best and develop our talents. This card indicates that future success will be hard-won, but ultimately we will reach greater heights as a result of this.

Interpretation

When this card appears in a spread, it is encouraging you to fight for what you believe in and defend your own values. The initiatives that you taken have provoked stiff rivalry and you have to prove that you are more than capable of handling this. You will need skill and resilience to deal with the opposition you are facing, but the Seven of Wands suggests that you have the ability to meet the challenges that are inherent in this card. You have the willpower, the courage and the perseverance to succeed, as well as the knowledge that you have already proven yourself. The path you have chosen has led you to this point and you now need to deal with the consequences of your choices. This will not be easy, but it is within your grasp.

Marseilles Tarot

Royal Fez
Moroccan
Tarot

Eight of Wands

The flying wands are
like arrows moving
toward their target

The tranquil
landscape foretells a
positive outcome

ACTIVITY ☾ TRAVEL ☾ NEW MOMENTUM
ROYAL FEZ MOROCCAN TAROT

The Eight of Wands indicates a time of excitement and movement. This
card represents action channeled in a positive direction. The inherent
fiery optimism of the suit of Wands, coupled with the benign
circumstances of this card, give rise to a feeling of positive anticipation.
Traditionally, eight wands are featured flying over a peaceful landscape.
The wands are in bud and are aiming straight for their chosen target.
The restlessness of the suit of Wands signifies that things are now
surging ahead to a new beginning.

Symbolism

The initiatives at the beginning of this suit have now gathered momentum. The Eight of Wands signifies movement towards a new goal—developments that encourage us to believe in the path we have chosen. This card marks a turning point, because we are now ready to move on after a period of delay. The Eight of Wands is an optimistic card, for it indicates that the way ahead is clear. We have resolved our anxieties and are set to focus on the journey ahead. As a result, our vision is clear and our intuition can flow freely. We can give expression to our ideas and successfully use our skills to further our aims and ambitions. The future is something to look forward to and we are filled with a sense of positive expectation concerning what lies ahead.

Interpretation

When you draw this card, you can expect things to start moving quickly. You have limitless enthusiasm for your current project and want to throw yourself wholeheartedly into it. The Eight of Wands marks a time of action, when you can put your ideas into motion knowing that the climate is favorable. Your creative energy is at its strongest and you are able to channel it productively. This may mark a period of advancement in your career or fruitful activity. Travel is sometimes indicated, because you are ready to broaden your vistas. New people may come into your life that reflect this expansive time. The Eight of Wands indicates success ahead, and that you should take full advantage of this productive phase.

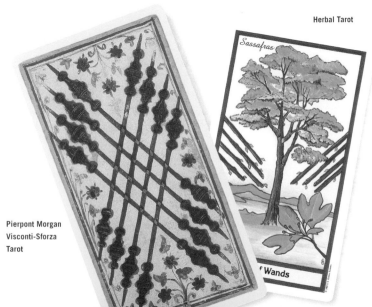

Herbal Tarot

Sassafras

Pierpont Morgan Visconti-Sforza Tarot

f Wands

Nine of Wands

The sailing ships are indicative of our ultimate survival

The warriors summon their strength for the battle that lies ahead

Nine of Wands

DETERMINATION TO SUCCEED ☾ STRENGTH IN RESERVE

MEDIEVAL SCAPINI TAROT

The Nine of Wands suggests that you have the strength to conquer a particular trial that lies ahead. Whatever adversities you have to contend with—and however daunting this particular obstacle—this card is telling you that you are equipped to survive. In the Morgan Greer Tarot, a man wearing a plumed helmet is poised to do battle for what he believes in. He holds a wand in his left hand, while eight more stand strongly behind him. He has the courage to confront whatever challenge awaits him, just as those facing battle in the Medieval Scapini Tarot do.

Symbolism

Although the odds look overwhelming and it is hard to see how to deal with a particularly daunting situation, the Nine of Wands indicates that we are close to the finishing line and just need to make one last superhuman effort. We may feel as if we have nothing left to give, but this card reassures us that we do have the fighting spirit to pull through. When the Nine of Wands is drawn, it reminds us that this is not the first challenge we have faced and that our resolve ultimately becomes stronger with each setback. The trials of the past—and the fact that we have come through them successfully—have put us in a stronger position than we may realize. No matter what the opposition, we know in our hearts that we will survive it.

Interpretation

Even though you find yourself daunted by what lies ahead, the Nine of Wands suggests that you have the powers of endurance to come through. You may feel that you cannot go on or that life is too difficult, but deep down you can draw on a formidable reserve of strength that will keep you going.

You have already overcome countless obstacles and, even though you are now facing even more difficulties, you are determined to win through. It is vital to conserve your energies and rely on your innate strengths. These reserves will come in very useful, not just physically but mentally and emotionally. Do not allow yourself to feel stuck; instead, keep your mind on what lies beyond the present impasse.

Morgan Greer Tarot

Golden Dawn Tarot

Ten of Wands

The armful of wands is too large for the man to carry

The burden is borne, but may in the end be just too great

TOO MANY RESPONSIBILITIES (DISILLUSIONMENT
MORGAN GREER TAROT

The Ten of Wands reflects the importance of learning the limits of what can and cannot be achieved. This card underlines the inherent pitfalls of the suit of Wands and what happens when the dictates of reality are ignored. In many decks this card depicts a man who is carrying ten heavy wands in his arms—often as he struggles uphill. He has overburdened himself and is now suffering the consequences. He needs to stop and examine what he truly can and cannot cope with and just why he has taken on too much.

Symbolism

Like its corresponding element of fire, the suit of Wands is full of enthusiasm. It is not surprising, therefore, that there is a great sense of disillusionment when we feel restricted in any way. This card underlines the danger of biting off more than we can chew. We may feel oppressed, but the message of the Ten of Wands is that, more often than not, this is self-imposed. It is up to us to find a way to relieve ourselves of our burden. In our ignorance of what we could and could not do, we may have borne too many responsibilities and the pressure is now beginning to take its toll. We need to consider how best to lighten the load and delegate or even let go of certain plans. A new creative cycle can begin once we have relinquished some ties.

Interpretation

When the Ten of Wands appears in a spread, it indicates that you have reached a point of exhaustion and cannot go on as you are. You may feel weighed down by excessive duties. It is important to understand why you feel so trapped, so that you can take responsibility for your position. The Ten of Wands reflects the fact that you need to be aware of your personal limitations—otherwise you will end up taking on more than you can cope with. It stresses the importance of knowing what to take on and what to turn down. You need to find strategies to help you to cope, such as sharing your load with others. It is vital to stop, re-evaluate your situation and then reorganize yourself so that you can feel inspired once more.

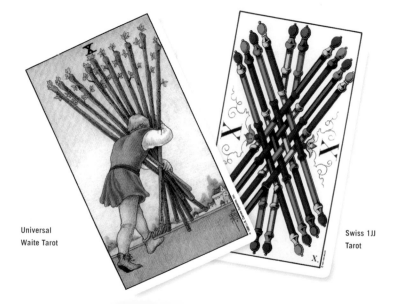

**Universal
Waite Tarot**

**Swiss 1JJ
Tarot**

Page of Wands

The ornate wand
signifies creative ideas

The Page's plumed
hat is a symbol
of his flamboyance
and confidence

PAGE of WANDS

INSPIRATION ☾ UNTAPPED POTENTIAL ☾ A FRESH START
SWISS 1JJ TAROT

The Page of Wands reflects the very beginnings of a creative process,
which will need careful input in order to realize its potential. All of
the Pages act as messengers, and the Page of Wands inspires us with
imaginative ideas. He (or, in the case of the Golden Dawn Tarot, the
Princess) is often shown wearing a decorative tunic or cloak and standing
in a fertile landscape holding a wand. He gives the impression of being
confident in his own abilities, and his youth is a symbol of untapped
potential and new possibilities.

Symbolism

We are beginning to glimpse our creative capacities when the Page of Wands appears. We sense that our lives are ready to open up and we want to put our ideas to the test. This card symbolizes a stirring from within that alerts us to our desire to grow and learn more about ourselves and others. The Page of Wands signifies that we are stimulated by the idea of a challenge and ready to grab any opportunities that come our way. This is another action card that inspires plenty of enterprise. We have enough faith in ourselves and in the project in question to see it through to the end. Ultimately, we may discover that, in our childlike enthusiasm, we have overestimated the viability of such an endeavor. But whether what we embark upon proves practical or not, much nurturing and assistance will be required in order to bring the tiny seed to fruition.

Interpretation

Drawing the Page of Wands means that you are on the threshold of a creative phase. You feel inspired to develop your innate talents and excited by the breadth of your vision. You have the self-belief to convert your dreams into reality, but you need to pay close attention to how you go about manifesting your vision. You will bring an element of light-heartedness to your endeavors, as well as an infectious enthusiasm. The Page of Wands can also represent someone who embodies energy, wit, and good humor and who brings some fun into your life.

Golden Dawn Tarot

Pierpont Morgan Visconti-Sforza Tarot

PRINCESS OF WANDS

Knight of Wands

The Knight looks
straight ahead at the
challenge that
awaits him

He has an air of
strength and
purpose about him

A MOVE ☾ A CHANGE OF HOME ☾ JOURNEYS
ROYAL FEZ MOROCCAN TAROT

The Knight of Wands represents the spirit of adventure that takes us

into the unknown. This card combines all the enthusiasm and vision of

the suit of Wands with the youthful, questing spirit of the Knight. Tarot

decks traditionally feature a handsome and imposing Knight riding a

beautiful horse or proudly striding forward. He generally wears a plumed

helmet and carries a budding wand, as the symbol of creative energy.

This card embodies many of the ideals of chivalry, but also warns

against acting without considering the consequences.

Symbolism

This card is often an impetus for change. The Knight of Wands is full of ideas that may not always be grounded in reality, but are enough to inspire us. When we are in tune with the message of this card, we can move mountains. If we have been stuck in a rut, we are able to break out. However, this card should warn us against acting impulsively. "Act first, think later" might be its motto, but this could lead us into hot water. The Knight of Wands infuses us with a strong desire to experience life in all its dimensions. We do not want to be held back in any way. If the Knight of Wands appears as a person, he will be charming, fun, and full of energy and daring; but he may also be volatile, unreliable, and unpredictable.

Interpretation

Choosing the Knight of Wands suggests that you are ready to make a significant move of some kind. You may be moving home or country, or simply filled with a desire for novelty. The Knight may represent someone who acts as a catalyst for these changes. You may have a strong impulse to do something creative or to learn more about philosophical or spiritual matters. Or you may simply feel adventurous and in the mood for new experiences and fun. You have the desire to expand your life and feel more alive. If you have been feeling trapped and unable to change your circumstances, then the dynamic energy of the Knight of Wands will give you the impetus to do things that you would never have dared to try before.

Russian Tarot
of St. Petersburg

Knight of Clubs

Aconite
(Poisonous Herb)

Herbal
Tarot

of Wands

Queen of Wands

The wand is the symbol of the Queen's authority

The Queen of Wands radiates warmth and power

QUEEN OF WANDS

GENEROSITY ☾ WARMTH ☾ OPEN-HEARTEDNESS
MARSEILLES TAROT

The Queen of Wands is a warm, open-hearted, talented, and strong-willed woman. She is sometimes linked with the fixed fire sign of Leo. This gives rise to a strongly contained creative energy, which is both sustainable and productive. The Queen usually sits proudly upon her throne (adorned, in Zolar's Astrological Tarot with a lion on either side). She often carries a sunflower in her left hand and in her right hand holds a wand, the symbol of her rulership and nobility. A black cat may sit at her feet, depicting her role as "queen of hearth and home."

Symbolism

The Queen of Wands is an energetic, capable woman, a loving wife and mother, as well as a gifted business woman. She is often known as the "queen of hearth and home." She is extrovert and her generous, sympathetic nature and love of life make her well loved. The fact that she can successfully run a home and develop her own interests makes her a formidable person in her own right. She is understanding of others, but if crossed she can fight like a lioness, hence her reputation as a wonderful friend but a formidable foe. She is also warm, loyal, and trustworthy and knows exactly what she wants from life. She is capable of translating her vision into something tangible and this can act as a powerful stimulus to action.

Interpretation

Choosing the Queen of Wands means that you are about to enter a more passionate and creative phase in your life. Even if this card represents the appearance of someone else who personifies her attributes, ask yourself whether you are ready to embody any of these qualities yourself. You are feeling strong, independent, and positive at this moment in time and you can put these feelings to good use. You may want to channel your creative energy into a work project or some other area of interest that inspires you. You are ready to showcase your gifts to the world. Bask in the love and admiration of friends and family around you and feel the power and strength that are burning through you.

Zolar's
Astrological
Tarot

Morgan
Greer Tarot

King of Wands

The flaming wand is the symbol of the King of Fire

The horse's stance represents action and great power

Knight of Wands

CONFIDENCE (ENTHUSIASM (WILLPOWER

THOTH TAROT

The King of Wands (who becomes a Knight in the Thoth Tarot) denotes a powerful man who is accomplished, confident of his own abilities and optimistic. He is both strong-willed and fair-minded and has a great capacity to motivate others. He exudes enormous power and authority and is traditionally shown either astride a galloping charger or seated on a wonderfully ornate throne and looking ready for action. He clasps a wand (often shown flaming or in bud), which suggests that he has tremendous power in his hands, which he must use carefully and wisely.

Symbolism

This card describes a man who has the courage of his convictions and a strong belief in himself. Like the Knight of Wands, the King is warm, charming, and sometimes foolhardy, with a talent for inspiring others to reach for the stars. He has a tremendous zest for life, and his imagination can encourage us to strive beyond our personal limits. When the influence of the King of Wands is strong, we feel optimistic and capable of living our vision. We are overflowing with exciting ideas and ready to go wherever our questing spirit will take us. We are also able to trust in our intuition. We may exemplify the spirit of leadership, and our strong-minded, authoritative approach to life will be inspirational to those around us.

Interpretation

Like all of the court cards, the King of Wands can be interpreted in two ways. You may be about to meet someone who typifies the characteristics of this card, or you may be ready to express these qualities yourself. If the latter is the case, then it is time to act on your intuition and move forward with confidence in what you are doing. Draw on your foresight and resourcefulness and make decisions that will further your ambitions in life. The King of Wands suggests that, provided you are able to deal with the practicalities involved, you can now achieve a tremendous amount. Your wisdom, knowledge, and natural exuberance will stand you in good stead and enable you to deal with any setbacks along the way.

Medieval Scapini Tarot

Golden Dawn Tarot

KING OF WANDS

King of Wands

Ace of Pentacles

The wings of spirit indicate that energy has the potential to manifest itself as something concrete

The hand emerging from the cloud symbolizes new ventures

ACE OF PENTACLES

NEW ENTERPRISE ☾ FINANCIAL PROPOSITIONS

GOLDEN DAWN TAROT

The suit of Pentacles (also known as Coins or Disks) corresponds to the element of earth. It represents worldly status, physical well-being, and financial security. The Ace of Pentacles indicates auspicious beginnings for financial propositions and business ventures. Traditionally, a hand emerging from a cloud offers a pentacle. In the Herbal Tarot, a garden lies below, indicating a reward for efforts made, and a long path leads to an arch in the distance, suggesting there is still a long way to go before the potential of this suit is realized.

Symbolism

The Ace of Pentacles symbolizes worldly success and material gain. This may be through our own efforts or as the result of a legacy or gift. Either way, we can expect a significant improvement in our financial circumstances. The time is ripe to give concrete expression to our skills and abilities and manifest them in the world so that we can achieve something positive with them. It marks the start of a project; in reality, nothing has yet materialized, but we feel good about ourselves and ready to initiate a fresh venture. This might take the form of creating a business, getting a new job, or establishing a home. There is every indication that we will be successful in our endeavors, which are likely to bring financial reward, prosperity, and security.

Interpretation

If the Ace of Pentacles appears in your reading, you can expect an increase in salary, a promotion, or the opportunity to gain more kudos at work. You are full of enthusiasm for the task in hand and have the necessary drive and determination to work toward fulfilling your ambition. You want to give yourself wholeheartedly, and your ingenuity and persistence will help you use your resources productively. This card gives your sense of self-worth a boost and results in your feeling solid in yourself. Your material circumstances are becoming better and you are feeling content. You are ready to enjoy the good things in life and indulge your physical senses. The Ace also sometimes indicates a strong family life.

Herbal Tarot

Swiss 1JJ Tarot

Ace of Pentacles

Two of Pentacles

Despite standing on
one leg, the young
man appears
perfectly balanced

The two pentacles
suggest the duality
of this card

FLUCTUATION ☾ BALANCE ☾ RESOURCEFULNESS
ROYAL FEZ MOROCCAN TAROT

The Two of Pentacles signifies equilibrium in the material realm,
as well as both emotional and financial security. A young man is generally
shown juggling two pentacles and, although the sea behind him may
be turbulent, he appears happy and light-hearted, for this card indicates
enjoyment of life. Meanwhile, he is managing to keep in motion both
poles—negative and positive—representing the fundamental duality
of this card: we are challenged to handle many different things
simultaneously and cope with various demands.

Symbolism

Balance is the most pressing issue when we choose the Two of Pentacles. We find ourselves having to juggle different needs and find ways of managing these conflicting aspects. This card indicates a great deal of activity and a time when we have to take on extra responsibilities. Sometimes the pressures of work or study conflict with our need for leisure time. Although harmony can be hard to achieve, the Two of Pentacles suggests that we have the necessary patience and endurance. We simply need to use our innate skills to cope with the irritations that crop up. If we adopt a calm, practical outlook, this will help things run smoothly. Even minor setbacks can be handled with good grace, provided we keep ourselves in check.

Morgan Greer Tarot

Interpretation

When the Two of Pentacles appears in a spread you are ready to start projects that offer a rewarding future, but you may feel anxious about the outcome and this could mark an uneasy time. You may need to keep several propositions going at once until you are sure which one is right for you. You will have to be skillful in the way that you go about the practical everyday matters of your life: changes are taking place in your financial circumstances and you must be flexible. This card indicates a period of fluctuation, when you need to weigh up the various factors involved in a new venture, if it is going to succeed. It is important that you put all your resources to work and actively take steps to promote your material prospects.

Pierpont Morgan Visconti-Sforza Tarot

Three of Pentacles

Added revenue from an unexpected source. Material success.

THE THREE OF PENTACLES

The church imparts a spiritual dimension

The architect signifies technical knowledge

MINOR ARCANA

Failure of a business proposal to materialize.

EFFORT BRINGS REWARDS ☾ TALENTS TO BE DEVELOPED
ZOLAR'S ASTROLOGICAL TAROT

The Three of Pentacles shows that the structure of a current project is complete. It is now necessary to concentrate on the finer details and add the finishing touches. Although this requires hard work and effort, a great sense of achievement will be gained. Zolar's Astrological Tarot features a mason or craftsman discussing plans with a priest and an architect: possibly ideas for the next stage of the work. The fact that this is being carried out in a church gives a spiritual dimension to his handiwork, which is needed for the ultimate fulfillment of the project.

Symbolism

The Three of Pentacles describes a situation in which we have dared to venture out into the world and apply our practical skills and can now confidently expect to attain our goal. This will happen slowly but surely, and we are well on our way to fulfilling our ambitions. We have now reached the first successful conclusion of a project and need to put some effort into keeping the momentum going. Although there is a strong sense of satisfaction at what has been achieved so far, there is still much to do. The approval of others buoys us up and we deserve all the praise we are given. The Three of Pentacles underlines the fact that hard work is still necessary, but everything is looking very promising.

Interpretation

Drawing the Three of Pentacles shows that your industry, application, and talents are paying off. You have a chance to show just what you can do and may gain some recognition for this. Success in exams, your career, personal projects, and business matters is indicated. You feel valued for what you can do and pleased with the groundwork you have laid for the future. There may be financial rewards for your efforts, or your sense of satisfaction may be felt on an inner level. This card suggests that you have the ability to bring your ideas to fruition. All you need is the willpower and determination to finish what you have started, and the Three of Pentacles suggests you have those qualities in abundance.

Medieval Scapini Tarot

Three of Coins

Thoth Tarot

3

Works

Four of Pentacles

Her calm expression
may mask a dangerous
complacency

The pentacle clutched
by the woman
signifiies possession

Four of Pentacles

STAGNATION ❧ NOTHING VENTURED, NOTHING GAINED
HERBAL TAROT

This card symbolizes "nothing ventured, nothing gained" and having

insufficient faith in the unknown. Some kind of action or risk is required

to keep things flowing on both a material and an emotional level. In the

Herbal Tarot, a figure sits with three disks in front of her and one above

her head. She holds one pentacle close to her and appears calm and

secure, but at the same time neither animated nor inspired. The warning

here is that although we may feel secure when we possess something,

the desire for material security can ultimately stifle our growth.

Symbolism

The Four of Pentacles describes an unwillingness to share our material or emotional resources. As a result, we become miserly with regard to money and love. We may be so comfortable with our circumstances that we become complacent. Although it is very pleasant to be financially secure, the desire to hold on to what we have can stifle growth and block creative energy, so that we stop moving forward and instead limit ourselves to what is familiar. When we put too much emphasis on the material realm, we may lack vitality and inspiration. Our over-cautiousness becomes an obstacle to further change and we become excessively possessive of what we have. We may even become suspicious of other people's motives. This card suggests a need to confront our fear of letting go and recognize why we are holding on so tightly to our possessions and emotions.

Interpretation

The Four of Pentacles in a spread may indicate that you are feeling bogged down by materialistic concerns. It warns of the dangers of being too possessive of your finances and your emotions— you need to share what you have, or you may become stifled by a lackluster approach to life. Your sense of self-value may be too dependent on what you own, and you may need to let go of certain things in order to re-evaluate yourself. This card suggests a good long-term financial outlook, provided you become more flexible.

**Russian Tarot
of St. Petersburg**

**Swiss 1JJ
Tarot**

Four of Coins

Five of Pentacles

The solid nature of the pentacles represents our ability to survive

This term suggests that the problem may lie in our minds as much as in actual reality

Worry

SPIRITUAL, EMOTIONAL, OR FINANCIAL LOSS
THOTH TAROT

A strong sense of loss accompanies this card. Money worries or other hardship, such as illness, may be indicated and it may be difficult to maintain a sense of purpose in life. Various Tarot decks offer variations on figures standing before a lighted church window that frames the image of five pentacles. It may be snowing and the figures usually appear poor, wounded, and destitute, although the church window is a symbol of hope and suggests that we can find security if we unite our spirituality with our material world.

Symbolism

The feeling of loss inherent in the Five of Pentacles may refer to our material and our emotional lives; something on which we place great value is in danger of being forfeited. We may be having financial difficulties, relationship problems, or a crisis of faith. We may doubt our abilities or feel we have lost our spiritual direction. However, we may be looking for support in the wrong place and have to reorientate ourselves. This card indicates the need to align ourselves with our inner spirituality. The more solid we are in our inner world, the more likely we are to feel secure in the external world. The Five of Pentacles reminds us that we have the resources, but need to find new ways of valuing ourselves.

Interpretation

The Five of Pentacles indicates that you feel over-extended and at a loss as to how to proceed. You have a sense of lack in your life, particularly a lack of something for which you feel a strong need. As a result, you may become unemployed or suffer a loss of income and feel great uncertainty; fear of poverty or illness may undermine your well-being. You need to pay great attention to the financial, emotional, and spiritual areas of your life. Moral support, love, and comfort are available, but they may not come from the direction you expect. You may have a sense of being on the wrong path or alienated from others, but this card urges you not to despair and to ensure you take care of yourself, on an inner and outer level.

**Morgan
Greer Tarot**

**Royal Fez
Moroccan
Tarot**

Six of Pentacles

The merchant represents the financial security embodied in the suit of Pentacles

The six coins indicate a sharing of our resources

Six of Coins

GENEROSITY ☾ FAITH ☾ KINDNESS

MEDIEVAL SCAPINI TAROT

The Six of Pentacles indicates a willingness and a desire to share good
fortune and success with others, and such generosity may in turn come
to be reciprocated. Frequently a merchant is depicted surrounded by
six pentacles. He may be handing over a coin to the outstretched hand
of an unseen person, as he is in the Herbal Tarot, signifying that
he is quite willing to share his wealth with others. He knows that
he must use his wealth ethically and spiritually and this is expressed
by the giving of what he possesses.

Symbolism

This is often thought of as a lucky card and signifies that everything is destined to turn out well for us. "What goes around comes around" is an apt saying for the Six of Pentacles and we can expect to receive what is rightfully ours. Financial help may be in the offing and—whether through our own efforts or fortunate circumstances—we will receive the help we need at just the right time. By the same token, we are feeling generous toward others and will want to show our appreciation: we may have the chance to fulfill a karmic obligation, clear a debt, or repay a favor. We are able to recoup our losses and regain our faith in human nature. This card marks a more ethical relationship with the material dimension of life.

Interpretation

When the Six of Pentacles appears in a spread, you know that you will soon be in a position to share your resources with others: you may be about to inherit some money, have a windfall, reap the financial rewards of your investments, or receive a gift. This is a time when you feel you can afford to extend yourself to others and be magnanimous. Equally, someone who is in a position of power or influence may help you. For example, you might be offered financial support for a business venture. You have a feeling of well-being and security and a sense that your endeavors will ultimately be successful. This is a moment to be charitable and generous in your actions, as well as to enjoy the kindness of other people.

Golden Dawn Tarot

Herbal Tarot

Seven of Pentacles

The bush of pentacles may represent a project or a relatiohship

The young man pausing in his work signifies a time of deliberation

© 1990 U.S. Games Systems, Inc.

A DIFFICULT DECISION ☾ PATIENCE ☾ COMMITMENT
UNIVERSAL WAITE TAROT

This card represents a choice that has to be made and certain decisions that need to be taken. A crossroads has been reached and a time of deliberation is required before taking the next step. The Universal Waite Tarot portrays a young man leaning on his staff while he quietly watches the pentacles growing like fruit. He seems to be assessing what he has been able to achieve so far and what now needs to be done to achieve further progress. He will eventually be required to act in order to reap the rewards of his labors.

Symbolism

The Seven of Pentacles depicts a situation where it is time to decide whether to stay on the tried-and-tested path or venture in a new direction. If we choose the latter, we may jeopardize everything we have managed to achieve so far, but this card warns against the dangers of complacency. We may be justifiably pleased with the degree of success that we have achieved to date, but at the same time fresh ideas are emerging that could bring us even greater accomplishments. It may be wise to pause for a while and consider the implications of developing our potential. We will need to put in consistent effort and put our practical skills to work, if our plans are to come to fruition. Everything hangs in the balance.

Interpretation

Choosing the Seven of Pentacles indicates that it is time to take stock. You may be in two minds about whether to abandon what you have been doing and try something completely new. The circumstances may look challenging at the moment, but you should not be discouraged by present setbacks. The message of this card is "Don't give up," because persistence will be worthwhile and will bring you the rewards you deserve. The Seven of Pentacles often marks a period of frustration when you are not sure exactly where to channel your energies. However, as long as you keep your focus and maintain your commitment, it indicates that you will eventually see your plans materialize.

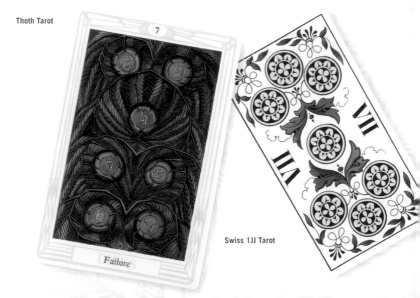

Thoth Tarot

7

Failure

Swiss 1JJ Tarot

Eight of Pentacles

The pentacles on the wall signifiy the fruits of the artist's labor

The carver hones his skill by creating the same shape time and again

DISCOVERY OF NEW TALENT ☾ DEVELOPMENT OF SKILLS

MORGAN GREER TAROT

The Eight of Pentacles is sometimes referred to as the "talent" card, representing an ability that needs to be developed in order to reach our full potential. It indicates great enthusiasm in discovering that we have more to offer than was previously realized. A contented-looking man is usually depicted carving pentacles. He is enjoying his work and proudly displays the results of his labor on the wall beside him. This represents the desire to express ourselves in life and acquire new skills and ideas that we can manifest in the world.

Symbolism

Satisfaction from the work we do and a sense of a progress in our career form the message of this card. We feel a deep sense of pride and personal enjoyment in the skills that we have at our disposal. We feel inspired to further our talents, and the Eight of Pentacles may indicate a readiness to return to study or begin an apprenticeship in order to acquire additional qualifications. Considerable effort will be required to build up a new career, but in so doing we will acquire extra knowledge and become better equipped. This card indicates not only material gain, but the emotional satisfaction that comes from knowing that we are fulfilling our promise. It may also suggest that we possess a multitude of talents or a specialized skill.

Interpretation

The appearance of the Eight of Pentacles suggests that you can put your talents to good use: you may be offered a new job, a promotion, or an apprenticeship to learn a skill that is relevant to a future career; you may be involved in a project that is an expression of your true nature. You are able to get pleasure from what you are doing—whether it is work or a hobby that you find emotionally satisfying. You may have an innate skill that you are able to market, or you may be going back to study at a stage in your life when you would not normally expect to change direction. Whatever your situation, you have a thirst for knowledge and are prepared to work hard to secure a solid foundation for the next phase of your life.

Zolar's
Astrological
Tarot

This card indicates a promotion. Improved financial opportunities.

Use your talents in legitimate channels only. Danger otherwise.

Pierpont Morgan Visconti-Sforza Tarot

Nine of Pentacles

The grouping of six
pentacles represents
a finished phase

The lush garden
signifies the woman's
harmony with nature

Nine of Coins

MATERIAL SUCCESS ☾ WELL-BEING ☾ CONTENTMENT
RUSSIAN TAROT OF ST. PETERSBURG

This card describes the immense satisfaction that is felt on achieving something of great personal significance and suggests the confidence to acknowledge our achievements. A beautifully dressed woman stands alone in a flourishing garden. In the Royal Fez Moroccan Tarot, a falcon sits on her gloved hand, symbolizing that her thinking is controlled.

The pentacles (or coins in the Russian Tarot of St. Petersburg) are shown in one group of six—meaning that a cycle has been completed—and a further group of three, signifying both movement and wholeness.

Symbolism

The meaning of this card is pleasure at what we have been able to achieve. We have a strong sense of uniqueness and a high level of self-esteem, based on the success of our efforts. We are confident in the knowledge that we have earned our rewards and this gives us a sense of long-lasting satisfaction. This card indicates the successful completion of something that leads to material comfort and happiness. We have achieved self-mastery, and the fact that we are not reliant on the approval of others to know our own worth gives us a sense of inner strength. We have reached a high point in our lives and can justifiably feel a sense of wholeness and gratification. This card indicates that we are content with our own company.

Interpretation

When the Nine of Pentacles shows up in a spread, it is a positive indication that everything is going according to plan. You are reaping the rewards of your endeavors and this gives you a wonderful feeling of happiness and security. You feel at peace with yourself and have reached a stage in your life where you feel good about who you are. You are in a position to truly appreciate the obstacles you have surmounted and take a well-deserved rest. You now have a solid sense of your identity and an appreciation of your talents. Sometimes this card indicates enjoyment of self-sufficiency and privacy. The deep satisfaction that you experience at last comes from your own sense of self and not from the validation of others.

Royal Fez Moroccan Tarot

Golden Dawn Tarot

Ten of Pentacles

The solid nature of the castle indicates a sense of all-pervasive security

The old man's environment is safe and comfortable

SECURITY (ABUNDANCE (LASTING HAPPINESS
UNIVERSAL WAITE TAROT

The Ten of Pentacles represents the culmination of everything that is inherent in this suit. It indicates feeling comfortable with who we are and having reached the stage to enjoy life to the full. The Universal Waite Tarot shows a lavishly robed old man sitting in the foreground of the picture. His family surrounds him and his dogs stand faithfully by his side. A sense of both material and emotional security radiates from the scene. The castle featured in this deck—and, traditionally, in others— looks solid and well established.

Symbolism

The Ten of Pentacles symbolizes the desire to create something permanent in our lives and signifies a strong urge for stability, such as the need to put down roots, buy a house, or start a family. It promises the satisfaction of achieving something worthwhile that will stand the test of time. We are able to recognize the value of what we have and feel a deep sense of material, spiritual, and emotional abundance. Sometimes it indicates that we can count on family support (both financially and emotionally) or that we are in a position to help others. Our relationships are stable, fulfilling, secure, and mutually beneficial. A transition—such as going from being single to being married—is another positive manifestation.

Interpretation

If the Ten of Pentacles appears in your Tarot reading, it indicates that you have reached a point in your life when something that is complete brings you emotional abundance and material security. It is a very auspicious card if you are moving house or starting a family. Sometimes a legacy— either in a literal or metaphorical sense—is the meaning of this card. Alternatively, you may be intending to make provisions for your family. If you are planning a business trip, this card indicates that it will be successful. However the Ten of Pentacles manifests itself in your life, you can rest content in the knowledge that you have been able to create something tangible that you can leave behind for future generations.

Herbal Tarot

Ten of Pentacles

**Medieval
Scapini Tarot**

Ten of Coins

Page of Pentacles

The intentness
of the Page's gaze
symbolizes total
immersion in his vision

The exotic landscape
implies the fruition
of an idea

IMPROVED FINANCES ☾ PROMOTION ☾ ADVANCEMENT

ROYAL FEZ MOROCCAN TAROT

All of the Pages represent new beginnings and need to be taken seriously
in order to bring something to fruition. The Page of Pentacles signifies
the slow but sure manifestation of a deeply held idea or vision.
The Page is normally pictured standing amid a lush landscape, which
is sometimes sprinkled with flowers. He is looking intently at the golden
pentacle that he is holding carefully in his hand. He is often dressed
in shades of green and brown, representing both the colors
of the suit of Pentacles and the element of earth.

Symbolism

This card suggests that we may be given an opportunity to start a career that holds great potential, or gradually turn a hobby into a lucrative income. Either way, we have a chance to build up our energy and resources in order to create something tangible. This Page indicates that we are developing our material values, but—as with all Page cards—we need to nurture this process, as it is still in its early stages. If this card represents a young person, then he will have respect for material things and be serious and diligent in learning new ideas—his ability to articulate a love of learning may even act as a catalyst for our own burgeoning ideas. This card suggests that we can make a success of an innovative venture, if we are willing to start at the bottom and work our way up. We are ready to take on a task that involves hard work, because we know that in the end it will pay off.

Interpretation

Choosing the Page of Pentacles suggests that money (albeit in small quantities) will be available to you. You may be beginning a new job that is initially routine but has excellent prospects. You need to be patient if you are to make a success of this opportunity—hard work will bring results. It is time to develop your material sense: this might happen through meeting a practical, earthy person who has a beneficial influence on you. This card promises long-term rewards in your finances, resources, and status, if you are open to good advice.

Zolar's
Astrological
Tarot

Morgan Greer Tarot

Knight of Pentacles

The reins signify passivity and caution

The calm nature of the animal suggests a state of contemplation

Prince of Disks

HARD WORK ❨ STEADY PROGRESS ❨ DILIGENCE

THOTH TAROT

The Knight of Pentacles (or Prince of Disks in the Thoth Tarot) represents the ability to set our sights on attainable goals and quietly persevere until they are reached. The capacity to work long and hard toward a chosen aim, even when this does not bring inspiration, is the gift of this card. Of all the Knights, this is the only one whose mount is standing still. They are in a freshly plowed or flower-strewn field and peacefully contemplate their surroundings. The reining in of the animal and natural reserve of pentacles make this Knight rather conservative.

Symbolism

Like all the court cards, the Knight of Pentacles can represent either a person in our lives or a quality that is ready to emerge in us. If it is the former, then he will be gentle, kind, sensible, pragmatic, and dependable. His down-to-earth nature, together with his ability to work hard, means that he usually achieves what he sets out to do. He applies himself patiently and, although he lacks great vision, knows what he is able to accomplish. His aims are modest and his caution make him a reliable, honest worker. He is prudent in his handling of finances, enjoys a quiet, simple life, and is happy living within his means. When this card symbolizes a quality, it indicates a positive outcome to a situation that may have appeared hopeless.

Interpretation

Drawing the Knight of Pentacles suggests that you are making steady progress toward your goals and that in time you will get where you want to be. Life often seems slow, with very little excitement or stimulus, but this may be because it is time to relax and enjoy the simple pleasures of life. Sometimes this card indicates that you are training for a new career, but that the work you are now doing is laborious or boring— don't lose sight of the fact that your prospects are good. Things may take longer than you wish, but your spirit of determination will win the day. If you meet someone who epitomizes the qualities of this card, it may mean that you are ready to manifest these qualities in the world.

Universal Waite Tarot

Golden Dawn Tarot

KNIGHT of PENTACLES

PRINCE OF PENTACLES

Queen of Pentacles

The Queen's serenity underlines her belief in herself

The lavishness of her clothes or her surroundngs indicates her prosperity and sense of well-being

QUEEN of PENTACLES

WEALTH ☾ GENEROSITY ☾ SELF-RELIANCE

SWISS 1JJ TAROT

The Queen of Pentacles is a practical, creative, efficient, trustworthy, warm, and sensuous woman. She loves the good things in life and is prepared to work hard to attain them. She is both comfortable in the world and a caring wife and mother. Traditionally, the Queen of Pentacles (or Coins in the Medieval Scapini Tarot) sits or stands serenely, often surrounded by the beauty of nature. She is in tune with everything around her and is completely absorbed in the good things of the earth. She enjoys life in all its many facets.

Symbolism

The Queen of Pentacles is in touch with her own nature and enjoys her position in the world. She believes in herself and gives happily of her resources. She commands respect because of her worldliness and material wealth, and is both giving and self-sufficient. Her physical surroundings are important to her, but she is equally happy amid the beauty of nature or in a lovely home. Her presence in a spread indicates material and emotional security and a strong sense of well-being: we may experience an increase in financial status or a more comfortable phase in our lives, both emotionally and physically. She also suggests that it is time to become more in tune with our bodies and our sensuality—we may need to pay more attention to our health and diet in order to feel more at ease. This Queen is attuned to the needs of others and we feel comforted by her presence.

Interpretation

Choosing this card suggests that you may need to adopt a more practical approach to material matters in order to secure a more comfortable way of life. You may need to be more self-sufficient or involved in the day-to-day running of your financial affairs. You are ready to immerse yourself in the good things in life and will be happy to share your luck with others. The Queen also denotes increased creativity. You may meet someone who engenders her qualities, or you may be ready to embrace her characteristics yourself.

Herbal Tarot

Medieval Scapini Tarot

Queen of Pentacles

Queen of Coins

King of Pentacles

The rod in the King's
right hand is the
symbol of his authority

The King of Pentacles
exudes self-mastery
and wisdom

WEALTH (STATUS (HARD WORK
GOLDEN DAWN TAROT

The King of Pentacles is a person of authority, who is respected for
his success and achievements. He is sensible and mature and always
honors his word. He is able to offer wise counsel and sound financial
advice, due to his expertise in this area. The King of Pentacles sits
contentedly on his throne or horse. He usually holds a rod of authority
in one hand and a large pentacle in the other. He is an imposing figure,
confident in his abilities and the knowledge that he has earned his
position and the respect that he commands.

Symbolism

The King of Pentacles is a stable, dependable, and practical person, who enjoys a high degree of security due to his material success. He naturally assumes an authority role and takes pride in his accomplishments and in the loyalty of those around him. He can make a significant contribution to an existing situation and his self-mastery and wisdom make him a born leader. He is in a position to carry out his ideas in a powerful but cautious manner. He also has excellent business acumen, is a tough but honest negotiator, and can teach others how to create abundance in their lives. He may be a skilled craftsman, as his strengths lie more in his practical nature than his intellect, and is able to give guidance without imposing himself.

Interpretation

If the King of Pentacles appears in your reading, it may signify that a wealthy, ambitious person is about to enter your life or that you are ready to develop your own desire for greater material security. You may meet a financial wizard who can advise you wisely. If so, he may well act as a catalyst for your own developing financial abilities and material self-confidence. This card heralds the successful outcome of a business venture and indicates that you have the energy to make a tangible success of your abilities: you are quite prepared to climb to the top of the mountain. The King of Pentacles suggests that you take a practical approach to your resources and learn to appreciate what you have.

Pierpont Morgan Visconti-Sforza Tarot

Marseilles Tarot

Ace of Swords

The golden crown is a symbol of attainment

The sword pointing directly upward represents commitment to the truth

UPSURGE OF MENTAL ENERGY (CONTROLLED ACTION
MARSEILLES TAROT

The suit of Swords embodies strong, forceful qualities that are connected with the intellect, but the Ace is a double-edged sword in that it cuts in both a positive and a negative way. All of the Aces mark new beginnings, and the Ace of Swords epitomizes the struggles that are inherent in this suit. In many Tarot decks an olive branch of peace and the palm of victory are shown emerging from a golden crown. The red and white roses that are portrayed in the Morgan Greer Tarot represent spirit and matter.

Symbolism

The masculine element of air, which represents the intellect, is linked with this suit. The Ace of Swords signifies our ability to think logically and act in a fair-minded, responsible way. It indicates a rational response to a situation of conflict or to differences of opinion. It denotes courage in adversity and reassures us that, although we may find ourselves in a situation in which everything looks hopeless, justice and truth will prevail. Conflict may be necessary in order to force us to look for new solutions to old problems, but we will be filled with a sense of strength, especially if we have to fight for something in which we believe. We are committed to the truth and are prepared to face difficulties because we have a strong sense that a resolution will be achieved. Drawing this card signifies that we understand our situation and can make sense of what we must do.

Interpretation

When you choose the Ace of Swords, you are in a position to deal effectively with a situation. Your mental powers are awakening and, although this may initially create conflict, the process will help you develop. You may have a revelation that informs your thinking. This card indicates the ability to plan ahead. If a situation requires action, you are able to be decisive, although you may be rather detached. You feel the need to involve yourself in circumstances where you can use your intellect, such as a high-powered job or some form of study.

Herbal Tarot

Ace of Swords

Morgan Greer Tarot

Two of Swords

The rocks represent the
reality of the situation

The sea symbolizes
the emotions

INDECISION ❲ REFUSAL TO FACE A SITUATION ❲ STALEMATE
UNIVERSAL WAITE TAROT

The Two of Swords signifies an impasse, in which nothing can either
move forward or change. There is great tension in this situation and
an uneasy balance between two equal but opposing forces. The Universal
Waite Tarot shows a blindfolded woman sitting at the water's edge
holding two swords that are perfectly balanced—at least for the time
being. The blindfold signifies that she is hiding from the truth
of her situation and ignoring both her emotions and reality
by refusing to look at anyone or anything.

Symbolism

Fear of upsetting the status quo is the meaning of this card. We may find ourselves in a situation in which we are unhappy but afraid to change. Refusing to face up to things creates tension and this card suggests that, however hard we try and blind ourselves to the truth, the storm must break and life will inevitably be disrupted. We may be able to maintain temporarily a false sense of stability, but this card indicates that the balance can be upset at any moment. Peace and quiet can only be maintained by self-restraint, but the equilibrium we are trying to sustain is far too volatile to hold in the long term. We may feel we are in a "damned if we do and damned if we don't" scenario—we cannot progress and we cannot escape. Sooner or later we need to pluck up the courage to confront the situation and trust that, once we have dared to address the issue, we will be able to break the deadlock.

Interpretation

The Two of Swords in a reading signifies that you will continue to feel trapped until you confront your fears. You may have reached an unsatisfactory point in an antagonistic relationship, yet be desperately trying to maintain a precarious balance. It is obvious that the tension will have to be faced, sooner or later. You are at a crossroads, and weighing up one possibility against another could simply deepen your indecision. The Two of Swords indicates that, once you have made a move, you will be able to see the way forward.

Golden Dawn Tarot

Russian Tarot of St. Petersburg

Two of Swords

Three of Swords

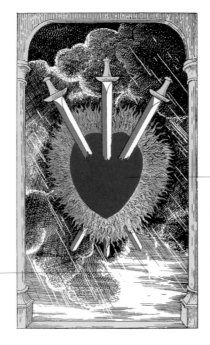

The pierced
heart represents
emotional upset

Lighter areas amid
the darkness offer a
ray of hope

DISAPPOINTMENT ❰ UPHEAVAL ❰ ENDINGS
ROYAL FEZ MOROCCAN TAROT

The Three of Swords describes a position that is full of pain, but
promises that a resolution is within sight. "The darkest hour is just
before dawn" is a saying that aptly depicts the psychological state
inherent in this card. In the Royal Fez Moroccan Tarot, dark skies, rain,
and clouds form the backdrop for a heart pierced by three swords,
indicating emotional suffering, although there is a glimmer of light,
suggesting hope. In the Thoth Tarot the dark, menacing background is
also pierced by lighter areas, but is accompanied by the word "Sorrow."

Symbolism

This card depicts a difficult situation that is reaching a climax, and there is an accompanying sense of relief that at last we are able to lance the boil. This is a necessary process and the understanding that is gained will help heal the wound. The Three of Swords offers us a sense of perspective on our current situation: we are able to see things in a more positive light, despite the fact that we may be going through dark times. We can no longer delude ourselves, and the insight we receive helps us to see things as they really are and puts our anguish into perspective. This card alludes to the fact that what we are going through is a prerequisite to our growth. Afterward we will be ready to wipe the slate clean and experience happier times.

Interpretation

When the Three of Swords appears in a reading, it indicates that it is time to clear away existing conflicts and make way for the new. You should understand that you have no choice: this is the only thing to do. Your realization that an ending must occur alleviates the inevitable sorrow you must experience. By being honest with yourself and coming to terms with what has gone wrong, you will be able to find a resolution and turn a negative situation into a positive one. Sometimes this card signifies an illness or medical procedure. You have a chance to learn about yourself, but this requires a long, hard look at the status quo. The changes involved may be distressing, but will make way for an auspicious outcome.

Thoth Tarot

Sorrow

Swiss 1JJ Tarot

Four of Swords

The four swords
indicate stillness
and recuperation
after a battle

This card suggests
that order and
structure are needed
in order to regroup

REST ☾ RECUPERATION ☾ RETREAT
PIERPONT MORGAN VISCONTI-SFORZA TAROT

The Four of Swords denotes the calm after the storm. It indicates
an opportunity to take a well-earned break after some struggles and
to recharge the batteries, either by choosing to spend time alone
or by having isolation imposed. Either way, it is exactly what is needed.
The Universal Waite Tarot shows an effigy of a knight lying on his
tomb in a church, his hands clasped in prayer. Three swords hang over
him and the fourth is fastened to his tomb. An air of complete stillness
and calm pervades the whole scene.

Symbolism

The Four of Swords indicates a phase of recovery after a period of emotional or physical turmoil. Often this means spending time alone in contemplation, so that we can come to terms with recent experiences. We need to think things through and may decide to get away from it all by going on a spiritual retreat or a holiday. Sometimes this card signifies recovery from an illness and the need to convalesce. We must recoup our energies and step back from recent painful experiences—if this has involved a loss, then the Four of Swords indicates a period of mourning so that we can begin to heal. Whatever our experience, this card suggests that we require a period of isolation so that we can prepare for a new dynamic to our lives.

Interpretation

Drawing the Four of Swords in a spread indicates that you would benefit from a period of mental relaxation. You may have been ill or recently have endured a stressful situation, and this will give you a chance to regroup and will give you the space to look after your emotional and physical needs. You have to recover your mental buoyancy and your physical vitality and the only way to do this is by taking time out. This is an excellent moment to look within and put recent events into perspective. It is important that you do not try and busy yourself with activities, as this represents an opportune time to put your house in order. It is only by being still that you will regain your equilibrium and be ready to enter the fray once more.

Medieval Scapini Tarot

Four of Swords

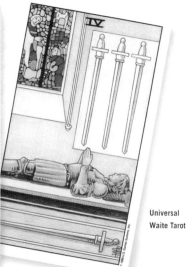

Universal Waite Tarot

Five of Swords

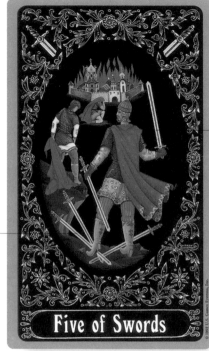

The upraised sword
symbolizes victory

The discarded swords
represent humiliation
and defeat

Five of Swords

FACING UP TO LIMITATIONS ☾ SWALLOWING PRIDE
RUSSIAN TAROT OF ST. PETERSBURG

This card represents arguments and hostility—and perhaps being
on the receiving end of someone's cruelty or vindictiveness. Although
there is a desire to strike back, the Five of Swords warns that there
is no alternative but to back off and admit defeat. Most Tarot decks
show a variation of a man standing victorious, having defeated two men
who are walking shamefully away. The victor seems omnipotent while
the vanquished have the air of being devalued and worthless, having
had no choice but to surrender their swords to the champion.

Symbolism

The message of the Five of Swords is acceptance of the inherent limitations of a situation and recognition that, no matter how resolute we are, we cannot change things—even though we may be tempted to fight our way out. Although we are powerless to alter the status quo, this card suggests that once we have reconciled ourselves to it, we can focus our energies on making a difference elsewhere. Often the Five of Swords imbues us with a sense of humiliation; we may feel worthless because someone has managed to get the better of us, or we have taken on something too large to handle. It is important that we stop banging our heads against a brick wall, for only then will we be able to face up to our responsibilities and move on.

Interpretation

When you draw the Five of Swords, it points to the need to accept the reality of things. Certain blocks are constricting you and you need to resign yourself to them before any changes can take place. It is not easy to accept defeat and swallow your pride, but this is the only tactic that will work. Trying to force things will only backfire and leave you feeling diminished. You may be feeling overpowered by circumstances, or a dominant person may be trying to control you in some way. You need to step back and realize that there is no point in trying to assert yourself, because the forces you are up against are stronger than you are. Sometimes this card warns against taking on too much and not being able to cope.

**Morgan Greer
Tarot**

Zolar's Astrological Tarot

Six of Swords

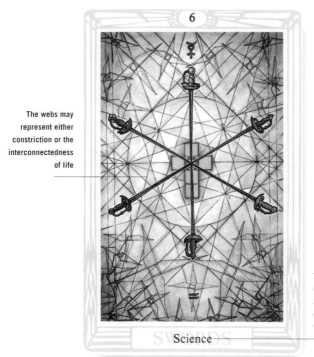

6

The webs may represent either constriction or the interconnectedness of life

The Thoth Tarot's designation of this card as the "Lord of Science" emphasizes its association with the intellect

Science

MOVING AWAY FROM STRESS ☾ DIFFICULTIES OVERCOME

THOTH TAROT

The harmony of the number six, combined with the innate difficulties of the suit of Swords, makes for an interesting mix. This card signifies a move away from turbulent times to a more peaceful state, although we are not out of the woods yet. The Royal Fez Moroccan Tarot depicts a man ferrying a boat to a distant shore—crossing the water indicating that past difficulties are being left behind. However, the swords in the boat imply that some old thought patterns still remain and that there is some anxiety about an unknown future.

Symbolism

The Six of Swords indicates that current tensions will be resolved. We have learned some of the lessons of the past and this gives us considerable peace of mind. The future is still unknown, but there are signs that circumstances are beginning to improve. Outdated thought patterns need to be relinquished, but this cannot be done overnight and will necessarily take time. This card denotes a new cycle, in which we have fresh hopes and expectations, as well as apprehension about what the future will bring. The journey we are taking may be an inner one, as we move from negative ways of thinking to more positive ones. We are now ready to overcome any obstacles before us, as we realize there is no going back but only moving forward.

Interpretation

If you choose the Six of Swords in your Tarot reading, then you may be ready to make a move to more harmonious surroundings or take a trip abroad. If this involves moving to a new location, this will mark a turning point and the start of a fresh cycle in your life. You have a much more positive outlook than in recent times and you are moving away—both mentally and physically— from the turbulent past, even though you know there may still be difficult moments ahead. You may have been through a period of great unhappiness, and this card underlines the fact that this will soon be behind you. You are now able to regain your dignity and self-respect after the humiliating experience of the Five of Swords.

Marseilles
Tarot

Royal Fez
Moroccan Tarot

Seven of Swords

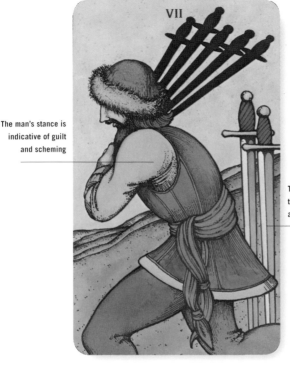

The man's stance is indicative of guilt and scheming

The two swords left in the ground symbolize a desire to be truthful

GUILE ❰ TACT ❰ DIPLOMACY
MORGAN GREER TAROT

The Seven of Swords calls for caution, guile, and evasion in order to reach an objective. Tact is required in a difficult situation, even though this may cause an uncomfortable feeling of not being true to ourselves. In the Morgan Greer Tarot, a man is seen making off with five swords over his shoulder, while two swords remain rooted behind him in the ground. He seems to be moving stealthily and furtively, as if he does not want to be caught. The picture has a quality of underhandedness, signifying that the man is not really happy with his actions.

Symbolism

This card indicates a necessity to be diplomatic and find a roundabout way of tackling things, rather than confront them head-on. We need to use our logical faculties to find an appropriate strategy to deal with the problem and get the best result. This may, however, leave us with an uncomfortable feeling, as our tactics may not be entirely above board. We might prefer to be more straightforward and honest, but the Seven of Swords suggests that to be successful, we now need to behave in a covert way. All we can do is have hope and faith that the end will justify the means. We will need to use all the intelligence and foresight embodied in the suit of Swords if we wish to secure an advantage—especially if we are dealing with a powerful opposition. However, we can pre-empt any trouble by being circumspect, patient, and willing to persevere.

Interpretation

If the Seven of Swords appears in a spread, it indicates the need to apply your mental energy in a very prudent way. This is not the time to behave aggressively. Instead, you should play your cards close to your chest and use diplomacy (or even subterfuge) to achieve the desired results. It might be loath to you to be economical with the truth, but this is necessary if you want to defuse the situation. If you are in conflict with someone or up against a difficult situation, then clear, logical thinking will help you through.

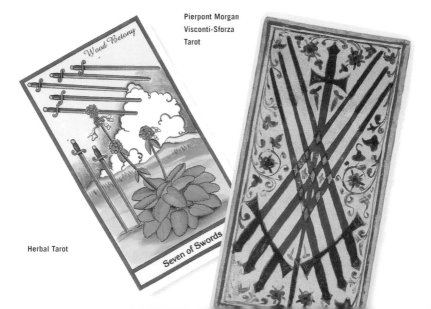

Pierpont Morgan
Visconti-Sforza
Tarot

Wood Betony

Herbal Tarot

Seven of Swords

Eight of Swords

Do not waste time on an unimportant issue.
When in doubt, do nothing.

THE EIGHT OF SWORDS

The castle represents
authority, but no one
is actually guarding
the woman

The fact that her legs
are not tied indicates
that only her fear is
keeping her imprisoned

You may start a new venture. Your worries
will prove unfounded.

FEAR OF BREAKING FREE ☾ INDECISION

ZOLAR'S ASTROLOGICAL TAROT

The Eight of Swords describes the need to choose between two equally
unappealing alternatives. This may be made all the more difficult by
temporarily losing sight of the circumstances. In various Tarot decks
a woman is portrayed standing tied and blindfolded in a marshy
landscape. Eight swords form a barrier around her (although the circle
they form is incomplete) and behind her stands a castle built on a rock.
She has lost sight of her situation, but her legs are still free, suggesting
that she is able to move forward if she chooses to.

Symbolism

The Eight of Swords depicts an unhappy situation from which we are afraid to extricate ourselves. We may fear the consequences of taking any kind of action, perhaps because we sense that things will not be easy—whatever we decide to do. We may feel trapped by our own indecisiveness, gripped by mental anguish, or oppressed by our circumstances, but we need to come to terms with the part we have played in creating them. We are still in a position to make some changes, albeit small ones. The situation may not be as complex as we think, but we need to face it as honestly as possible. Once we begin to take responsibility for our lives and break free from whatever is inhibiting us, we will begin to feel more empowered.

Interpretation

Drawing this card indicates that you feel hemmed in by circumstances. Even though these may be self-created and not as restrictive as you think, you may feel at a loss as to how to change them—paralyzed by your own fears and unable to act. You need to think rationally in order to find a way to free yourself from your mental imprisonment. The Eight of Swords warns against becoming too rigid in your outlook. You may need to confront an old behavioral pattern or a belief that is keeping you in such an inhibiting situation. The more you are able to do this, the easier it will be for you to see why things are the way they are. Be open and receptive and don't be afraid to ask for help. Sometimes this card also indicates stress-related problems.

Golden Dawn Tarot

Russian Tarot of St. Petersburg

VIII

Eight of Swords

Nine of Swords

The swords signify
mental anguish
and turmoil

The calmness of the
figure implies inner fears

Nine of Swords

ANXIETY ☾ DESPAIR ☾ NEGATIVE THOUGHTS
MEDIEVAL SCAPINI TAROT

This is traditionally known as the "card of nightmares," because the fears
it describes can be terrifying—even though they are not real. A sense
of impending doom often accompanies the Nine of Swords, but
it is important to separate our fears from the reality of the situation.
The Medieval Scapini Tarot depicts a figure lying on a coffin; nine
swords are hanging at right angles ominously overhead, but the figure
remains calm, implying that the fears are not external but lie within us.
Other decks portray bound hands, a weeping woman, or a dead animal.

Symbolism

The sense of gloom inherent in this card is more in the mind than in actuality. We may be feeling unduly pessimistic, or we may be caught in the aftermath of a difficult situation that continues to haunt us and color our perception of the future. What we most fear is unlikely to come true and things are never as bad as we imagine, but the pain we have experienced is painting everything black. We may be having bad dreams or morbid fantasies; or we may find it impossible to relax because we are feeling depressed. It might be helpful to uncover the actual source of our fears, since any insights that we gain will be helpful in dispelling them. Once we realize they are entirely unfounded, we will be able to enjoy ourselves again.

Interpretation

The Nine of Swords suggests that you are feeling overwhelmed by inner doubts that do not in fact have any bearing on reality. You may feel anguished and upset, but in truth there is nothing to fear. You might have to make a difficult decision or face a challenging situation, but the worries that grip you are far worse than the actual outcome. Negative thinking is exacerbating the situation, but sooner or later you will have to face the facts. Your circumstances will feel far less frightening when you are prepared to let go of your obsessive thoughts and are no longer controlled by them. Once you have adopted a new mindset, you can open your eyes to fresh opportunities and heal any health issues that are related to stress.

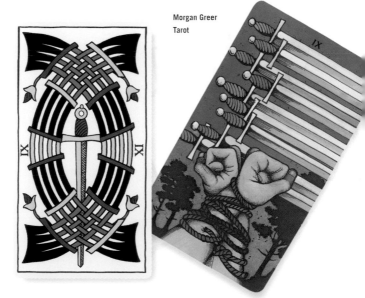

Morgan Greer Tarot

Marseilles Tarot

Ten of Swords

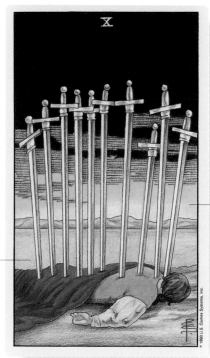

The dawn offers
the possibility
of a fresh start

The tranquil water
suggests that
everything is not as
turbulent as it seems

AN INEVITABLE ENDING ☾ PROMISE OF A NEW BEGINNING
UNIVERSAL WAITE TAROT

The Ten of Swords signifies the necessity to consider circumstances carefully before making a clean break. Once all the loose ends have been tied up, a new future with less conflict and struggle can be created. Many Tarot decks feature a figure lying face down in a barren landscape with all ten swords thrust into him—he is clearly dead; alternatively, ten bloodied swords may be thrust into the earth. Beyond the lake, the dawn is beginning to break, suggesting that a new beginning is in sight, however faint it might appear.

Symbolism

This card describes the resolution of a painful situation. Although we may have suffered great distress, we are now in a position to make a fresh start. The scales have fallen from our eyes and at last we are able to see things as they truly are. The fact that we now have clarity and perspective will help us to bear the grief and understand the necessity of letting go. We will be able to come to terms with an ending that is essential in order for new ideas and relationships to develop. Although we may not yet be able to see light at the end of the tunnel, a rebirth is promised us. Changes of this kind are never easy, but our ability to cope with them will make us realize just how strong and capable we are.

Interpretation

When you choose the Ten of Swords, one phase of your life is concluding and another will soon be beginning. There is a sense of inevitability, even if the change has been forced upon you. This card often marks the end of a relationship, when you let go of all your illusions and see the other person for what they really are. Although this can be an uneasy process, it signifies release from whatever has been holding you back. This might be a relationship, a work situation, or a way of thinking. The Ten of Swords marks a crisis point, but indicates that everything will improve. Learning from your experience will help you to move forward with greater optimism. Once you have hit rock bottom, the only way to go is up.

Herbal Tarot

Royal Fez Moroccan Tarot

Ten of Swords

Page of Swords

The Page's vigilance may occasionally turn into ruthlessness

The youthfulness of the Page suggests that he may act impetuously

PAGE OF SWORDS

GOSSIP ☾ INTELLIGENCE ☾ QUICK-WITTEDNESS
MARSEILLES TAROT

The Page of Swords (or Princess in the Thoth Tarot) is the messenger of the element of air. He is a master of words and signifies the emergence of novel ideas and means of expression. As with all the Pages, the potential to think in new ways is still in embryonic form. In the Marseilles Tarot, the Page of Swords appears to be standing on guard, brandishing a sword and checking that he is not in danger of attack. As he is a youthful figure, he may not have learned how to use his sword properly, warning against reacting clumsily to a situation.

Symbolism

If the Page of Swords represents a young person in our lives, he is likely to be alert, quick-minded, versatile, and strong-willed. His adaptable mind means that he is aware of different possibilities and has many varied interests. At best, he is a clear thinker who is well informed, fair-minded, and able to cut to the chase; he is resolute and his sharp intelligence enables him to make quick decisions. This makes him a very useful person to have around when we need to resolve a dispute. At worst, he is a gossip and deceitful; he can also be cold, ruthless, and aloof. This card sometimes warns us against jumping to conclusions without thinking things through—we need to guard against acting impetuously or inappropriately.

Interpretation

This card indicates that you will have to make some careful decisions that require clear thinking and level-headedness. It is important to keep a proper sense of perspective. Someone who is spreading rumors may complicate your circumstances, and you need to know who you can trust and who you cannot. You may meet someone who is in a position to keep you informed so that you can get the measure of things. The Page of Swords often signifies that you are mentally restless and eager to look at life in a fresh and more open way. You might meet someone who has an intellectual bias and who acts as a catalyst for this process. If you are signing a document or contract, make sure that you check the small print.

Pierpont Morgan Visconti-Sforza Tarot

Thoth
Tarot

Princess of Swords

Knight of Swords

The upraised sword is ready for the cut and thrust of battle

The boys pulling the chariot lead the Prince of Swords on his quest for change

PRINCE OF SWORDS

DRAMATIC CHANGE ❨ NEW PERSPECTIVES ❨ UPHEAVAL

GOLDEN DAWN TAROT

All of the Knights are on some kind of quest, and the Knight (or Prince) of Swords seeks intellectual stimulation and knowledge. He traditionally signifies conflict and is the most forceful and assertive of the Knights. In Zolar's Astrological Tarot, the Knight of Swords charges across the card, his horse's legs outstretched and its mane flying in the wind, highlighting speed and swift action; the Knight leans forward in his saddle, his sword raised high in the air, while in the background the wind has bent the cypress trees, symbols of sorrow and pain.

Symbolism

The Knight of Swords suggests that we are entering a mind-expanding time when our lives can change suddenly and our everyday pattern is disrupted. If he represents a person in our lives, he is likely to be courageous, intelligent, and able to deal with difficult situations. He is forthright in the way he confronts obstacles and can deal with opposition swiftly and effectively. He has an unemotional and sometimes ruthless quality which, although not intentional, can cause distress to others. He is not afraid of conflict and can successfully bring about a positive resolution, although his harsh words may cut to the quick and create disarray. Sometimes this card warns that flying off the handle will land us in trouble.

The Knight of Swords has a brilliant mind and is astute in making business judgments. We often meet him when we are ready to change direction.

Interpretation

If this card appears in your spread, you are ready to expand your mental faculties. Ultimately, this will lead you to a more expansive vision: you might move home suddenly or leave your job in the desire to take on a new challenge. Sometimes the Knight of Swords indicates conflict, and although this will not be easy to deal with, he suggests that you will win through. The more rational you can be, the easier it will be to resolve things. You may find yourself swept along by an exciting event, but the Knight warns that it could fizzle out very quickly.

Zolar's
Astrological
Tarot

Morgan
Greer Tarot

Queen of Swords

Her upright bearing
indicates her ability
to bear life's sorrows

The Queen's solitariness
may indicate that
she is a widow

STRENGTH (INDEPENDENCE (COURAGE IN ADVERSITY
PIERPONT MORGAN VISCONTI-SFORZA TAROT

The Queen of Swords is a symbol of intelligence, self-reliance,

determination, and willpower. She is a woman who can bear life's trials

and tribulations without complaint and shows great courage in adversity.

Traditionally, the Queen of Swords sits or stands alone, her posture

proud and erect. In the Universal Waite Tarot she wears a cloak patterned

with clouds and the throne she sits on is carved with butterflies, birds,

and angels—all linking her to the element of air. She solemnly holds her

sword upright and does not appear to notice the storm clouds gathering.

Symbolism

Traditionally the Queen of Swords is associated with a sense of sorrow or disappointment. She is able to suffer loss and loneliness with stoicism and knows what it is to stand alone in the face of adversity. She may be on her own by choice, for she values her independence and is resilient when dealing with disappointments. She has learned from her unhappiness and is more sure of herself as a result. The Queen of Swords—educated, clear-thinking, and both talented and ambitious in business—may be more comfortable as a career woman than as a mother or wife, although this card also signifies a divorcee or widow. She is respected for her analytical powers and has a brilliant capacity for judging a situation fairly and having an unbiased opinion. If we meet someone who embodies her qualities, it may be because they are naturally emerging in us.

Interpretation

Drawing the Queen of Swords may signify a need for her qualities of patience and courage in dealing with difficult circumstances. Alternatively, you may meet someone who epitomizes the Queen and is in a position to help you. This card suggests the need to learn through the inevitable ups and downs of life. The Queen of Swords is wise as a result of the difficulties she has gone through, and you may be asked to acquire these qualities, especially if you are going through a bad patch. It may be time to become more assertive.

Russian Tarot of St. Petersburg

Universal Waite Tarot

Queen of Swords

QUEEN of SWORDS

King of Swords

The King's upright sword symbolizes truth and right action

He looks calm and assured, giving the impression of an inner strength

King of Swords

JUSTICE ❨ ETHICS ❨ COMPASSION
HERBAL TAROT

The King of Swords has a strong regard for truth and justice and follows a sound ethical code. He is a formidable opponent as well as a tremendous ally. He also has an innovative mind and is a brilliant strategist. Sometimes we meet him in a person who acts as a catalyst for these qualities, which are emerging in our own psyches. The King of Swords is usually depicted in different Tarot decks as a powerful ruler dressed in armor, sometimes with a crown atop his helmet, as shown in the Swiss IJJ Tarot.

Symbolism

The King of Swords is a powerful advocate for fairness and equality. He is a respected authority figure, a natural leader, and a gifted negotiator, and makes excellent use of his intellectual skills when forging a professional path. Although he can be uncompromising, he is also diplomatic and trustworthy and has a strong moral code. He also likes to initiate projects and do things his way. However, his intellectual approach and propensity to control his emotions can cause him to appear cold and uncaring; he may lack compassion and be more successful in business than in personal relationships. This King has great strength of character and indicates that we are ready to develop some of his qualities for ourselves.

Interpretation

Drawing the King of Swords indicates that you may be about to meet someone who is powerful, ethical, and analytical, and who may open you up to a new perspective on life or give you a helping hand. This could lead to professional advancement in the form of promotion, to a honing of your intellectual skills, or to help with a legal or business matter. Alternatively, you may need to rely on your own mental acuteness and strength of character in order to cut through any difficulties. It may be wise to detach yourself emotionally from a current problem so that you can get a clearer vision and cope more successfully. When you choose the King of Swords, it may be advantageous to develop your powers of reasoning.

Medieval Scapini Tarot

Swiss 1JJ Tarot

KING of SWORDS

...ing of Swords

The Minor Arcana at a glance

No pictures appeared in the Minor Arcana until the Hermetic Order of the Golden Dawn started this tradition. The imagery of the Waite/Smith collaboration has since inspired many different approaches to the interpretation of the Minor Arcana.

The full Minor Arcana of the Universal Waite Tarot shows the 56 cards arranged in their respective suits. This pack is both contemporary and at the same time very close to the original deck that was designed by Arthur Waite.

Wands   Swords   Pentacles   Cups

Preparing for a Reading

This section looks at various simple guidelines that you
should follow in preparing for a reading. As you become
more experienced at using the Tarot, you will find your
own particular way of getting in the correct frame of
mind to read the cards, but it is always important to
create the right atmosphere. It will be difficult to attune
yourself to the meaning of the cards and to focus on the
reading if you are feeling distracted or agitated. An
ordered, established routine provides a secure framework
within which to work and will make you feel more
confident and relaxed.

The Oswald Wirth Tarot was created by a disciple of Eliphas Lévi, who sought to connect the Tarot with the Kabbalah.

Choosing a pack

There are many different kinds of decks from which to choose—only a few of which have been featured in this book. Some of the most popular and best known are the Universal Waite, Marseilles, and Thoth packs; some of the more unusual packs that are in use include the Mythic Tarot, the Tarot of the Witches, and the Ukiyoe Tarot. All of these decks are based on mythological, philosophical, and spiritual themes.

When you are choosing a deck, there are specific points that you should bear in mind. If you are buying your own pack, it is important that it has a strong visual appeal that stimulates your imagination and "speaks" to you in some way. If you get the chance to view a sample deck, have a look at all of the cards and see if they appeal to your sense of color, style, and imagery. The type of pack that you choose will depend to a large extent on how you intuitively respond to the cards, as well as on your own background and particular interests. It is, however, important to use a Tarot deck of your own and not one that belongs, or has belonged, to someone else. It is not possible to imprint your own psychic vibration on the cards and make them personal to you if someone else has

QUEEN OF CUPS

The Ukiyoe Tarot features traditional Japanese symbolism and figures in historical costume.

already colored them with their own energetic imprint. Selecting the pack yourself will help you develop your

intuitive (and perhaps even your psychic) abilities;
it will also attune you more successfully when you
give a reading.

Each Tarot pack has its own history and design and
has evolved in a unique way, but although the pictorial
images of the cards can vary considerably, the essential
meaning remains the same. If you are a complete
beginner, it is best to use a fully pictorial Tarot that has
the Minor as well as the Major Arcana illustrated.
Because the Tarot images are symbolic, each aspect of
the image has a particular meaning. You will need to
familiarize yourself with the more common and
traditional symbolism of the cards, as well as with the
unique symbolism relating to the pack of your choice.
It is important to start with a standard 78-card deck
(comprising 22 Major Arcana cards and 56 Minor
Arcana cards), and not with one of the decks based on
the Tarot but used more for fortune-telling purposes.

**Starting with a standard 78-card
deck will help you to familiarize
yourself with the deeper meaning
and uses of the cards.**

Setting the scene

It is always important to adopt an attitude of respect for the sacred images that are portrayed on the Tarot cards. This will enable you to connect more deeply with their meaning and symbolism. Ideally, you need to create a quiet, peaceful atmosphere before you begin a reading, so disconnect the phone and ensure that no outside distractions will disturb you. You may want to play some soft music, light a candle or some incense, recite a ritual invocation, or repeat an affirmation or prayer. Taking a few deep breaths can be a very calming way of letting go of extraneous thoughts and stilling the mind, or you may wish to do a short visualization or meditation. However you set the scene, it is important that you find your own way of creating a sacred space. Ritual is a simple way of creating the right mindset, and helps to establish a formal context for the reading and a secure focus for your thoughts.

When the stage is set for the reading, the person who is consulting the cards (the questioner) needs to think carefully about the

Lighting a candle is one of the rituals that you can perform to create an atmosphere conducive to a reading.

Establishing what the questioner hopes to discover is important, as it gives the reading a clear focus and provides a framework for interpreting the cards.

question on which they are seeking advice. Sometimes it is useful to write it down, because this helps to focus the concentration. If you are conducting the reading for someone else, it is not essential for you to know the question, but it is helpful to know whether it requires a yes/no answer or whether a choice between various different options is involved. Make sure that the questioner always phrases their query in a simple way. For instance, a question such as, "Will I get married or will I stay single?" is confusing—if the answer is "yes," does this mean: yes, you will get married; or yes, you will stay single?

Invite the questioner to shuffle the cards and to focus on their question while they are doing so. This will help to create a link between their inner dynamic and the pack. When they have finished shuffling, ask them to cut the deck and hand the cards back to you. When a question is asked, the Tarot will address not only the question itself, but everything connected to it. It will identify what is working for and against the questioner, as well as the optimum way to move forward. It takes time to become fluent in the language of the Tarot and the best way to develop your knowledge and expertise is to do some practice readings.

Allow your intuition to be guided by the cards, bearing in mind both the question and the symbolic meanings of the various images.

Synchronicity and practice

Before you begin a reading, give the deck to the questioner to shuffle and ask him or her to think of a question.

Many different spreads exist and more are being created all the time. Some use the entire deck to look at the questioner's life; others address specific issues, such as career and relationships.

The pictures and symbols of the Tarot are a way of helping us to express the language of the unconscious, and when we consult the Tarot, we open ourselves to this rich inner world. As we access this part of ourselves in a reading, it speaks to us in picture language and shows us—through symbols—what is at work deep within us. In other words, the Tarot reveals through its symbolic language whatever we are ready to become more aware of within ourselves. The synchronicity at work in a Tarot reading is such that we somehow choose exactly the right cards to reflect our particular situation. Our inner and outer selves are two sides of the same coin and at the time of a reading we

are offered a glimpse of the mysterious workings of the psyche through the cards that we select. The secret of understanding the Tarot is to be receptive and let its symbolism work in you. By going beyond the traditional meaning of the cards, we begin to connect with what lies beneath the surface of our everyday, conscious awareness. The creativity and inspiration of this deeper part of our being can guide us to greater self-knowledge and a more profound understanding of our life's path.

Once you have decided what spread you are going to use *(see pages 187–203 for some examples)*, shuffle and cut the deck and then deal the appropriate number of cards, laying them face down according to the pattern of your selected spread. Then turn them face up one at a time. (If you are using reversed meanings, which some people use to give different interpretations—that is, if the card is dealt upside-down—make sure that you turn the cards from side to side and not from end to end, otherwise you will reverse them.) Before you begin to interpret the individual cards, examine their overall balance and see how they relate to each other as a whole. Begin to absorb the general flavor of the reading: is there a sense of happiness and growth or of disappointment and difficulties? Are there more Major Arcana cards than you would expect (a normal ratio is three Minor Arcana cards to every Major Arcana card)? Does one particular suit dominate? All of these features have their own significance and will give added depth to your reading. Allow your intuition to tap into the meaning of the cards, bearing in mind the overall pattern of the spread and how the cards lie together.

Reading for a friend

Prince of Wands

If a card appears that does not seem to bear any relevance to the question, it needs to be carefully assessed to see what is trying to make itself known.

Like any skill, learning to read the Tarot requires practice. As you become more experienced, it will come more naturally to you.

It is important to remember that Tarot readings do not offer definite answers, but simply one perspective on a given situation. The overall meaning of the cards may offer an insight into the underlying reason for a particular situation but, ultimately, it is what we ourselves do with the information that determines the outcome.

Doing a reading for a friend gives you the chance to practice interpreting the cards in an informal way. Start off with a fairly specific question that is relatively easy to address. Occasionally, a Tarot reading will address a totally different question from the one being asked, perhaps because the questioner has not been willing to confront that particular subject. Be guided by your intuition and the guidance that the cards offer. The more you allow the symbolism of the cards to "speak" to you and inform the reading, the better your interpretation is likely to be. The relationship between the reader, the questioner, and the selected cards is a highly complex one, but provided that the atmosphere is conducive to the reading—and that both you and the questioner are open to the wisdom of the Tarot—it has the potential to give meaning and purpose to the experience.

Case Histories

A spread refers to the pattern in which the cards are laid
out and the order in which they fall. Some spreads help
you to gain a general overview of your life, while others
are more specific. For instance, the three-card spread
addresses just three particular areas, whereas the Celtic
Cross gives an impression of the current situation, the
inner and outer influences, and the psychology of the
questioner. Experiment to find the spreads with which
you are most comfortable. The longer you work with the
Tarot, the more you will intuitively choose the right
spread for a particular situation.

The Celtic Cross

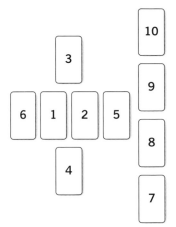

The Celtic Cross is one of the best known and most popular Tarot spreads. It provides an overview of the questioner's particular situation and is helpful as a general reading, as well as in answering specific questions. It consists of two parts: a small cross and an upright, or staff, typical of the Irish standing cross. This spread can be laid out using cards selected just from the Major Arcana or, as here, with cards chosen from the entire deck.

After the cards have been shuffled and cut, lay them out in the order shown above. Cards 1–6 form the cross and the vertical line to the right is formed with the four remaining cards.

Although each card has a specific position that determines its interpretation, you need to synthesize the meaning of the whole spread.

Case history

BRIAN

PHOTOGRAPHER

When Brian, 51, came for a reading he was working as a professional photographer. He was no longer feeling fulfilled in his career and wanted a change. His real passion was music and he was an accomplished pianist. His ambition was to work full time as a musician, but he was concerned about whether he could make a living this way. He hoped that the reading would shed some light on his dilemma.

Position 1: Present Position ✦ The *Tower* shows that Brian feels bound by a false image and finds it increasingly hard to live within the confines of his career.

Position 2: Immediate Influences ✦ The *Nine of Swords* describes Brian's anxieties about leaving the security of his established career. It is important to emphasize that these fears, although understandable, are ungrounded.

Position 3: The Questioner's Life ✦ The *Chariot* in this position reflects the conflict that Brian is experiencing as he struggles to make a decision.

Position 4: Root of the Reading ✦ The *Devil* suggests that it is up to Brian to break free of his self-imposed limitations, otherwise he will remain trapped.

Position 5: Past Influences ✦ The *Eight of Swords* implies that Brian has been feeling very restricted by his job. He needs to be patient and strong.

Position 6: Future Influences ✦ The *Seven of Wands* indicates a challenge that Brian has to overcome. Courage will be needed to meet this challenge.

Position 7: The Questioner's Feelings ✦ The *Star* is the wish-fulfillment card and indicates a new life in the offing. Brian can now see light at the end of the tunnel.

Position 8: Outside Influences ✦ The *Queen of Pentacles* describes the qualities of Brian's wife. It indicates that she will be a strong source of support for him and will help him to launch his new career.

Position 9: Hopes and Fears ✦ The *Hanged Man* indicates Brian's fears of sacrificing his security. It also suggests that he will gain something of greater value.

Position 10: Outcome ✦ The *Fool* predicts a fresh start for Brian and an opportunity to develop his potential. This will necessitate taking a leap of faith.

The Three-Card Spread

| 1 | 2 | 3 |

You can create a spread to answer any question. Simply decide what each card will represent, then shuffle the cards and lay them out.

The Three-Card Spread can be used in many different ways. In the example shown here the three cards represent the past, the present, and the future. However, you can invent your own categories, such as health, career, and love life; or the way forward, hopes and fears, and the outcome.

This three-card spread addresses three very specific areas of the questioner's life— past, present, and future—and gives a clear indication of the different influences at work.

Case history

Joy

NURSE

Joy, 28, had been living with her partner for five years. They had planned to get married and were in the middle of planning the wedding when he called the whole thing off. Joy was devastated and hoped that the Tarot reading would give her some insight into her upsetting circumstances.

Position 1: The Past ✦ The *Eight of Cups* indicates that some kind of upheaval in Joy's relationship was inevitable, since this card often indicates the end of a relationship. Joy now feels disillusioned and depressed, as well as powerless to change her partner's decision. Although she has not come to terms with the painful circumstances of her separation, this card suggests that she must let go and start to make sense of why her relationship did not work out.

Position 2: The Present ✦ *Death* in this position gives a very strong indication of the finality of Joy's relationship. It marks the end of one phase of her life and, although she is not ready to contemplate a new beginning, this is nevertheless on the cards. She needs courage to face the fact that she can no longer hold onto the past. A complete transformation is being offered and life will never be the same again.

Position 3: The Future ✦ The *Wheel of Fortune* reminds us that we are not always in control of the events of our lives. Fate has already intervened in Joy's life and this card suggests that more surprises are in store. Although the shock of her relationship breaking up was a "bad" surprise, part of her feels quite excited to think that she is in the throes of such dramatic change. This card tells us that nothing can stay the same for ever and that to progress we sometimes need to let go. Knowing that she needs to go down in order to come up again gives Joy a sense of hope and a realization that something greater is at work in her life. This does not detract from her bitter disappointment, but it does give her a sense that the ending of her relationship may have had a higher purpose.

The Horoscope Spread

This layout resembles that of the zodiacal houses and is a very useful spread for looking at all the different areas of someone's life.

The 12 houses and the 12 cards give specific insights into what is at work in each area of life at the time in question. The cards should be laid out in a counterclockwise direction.

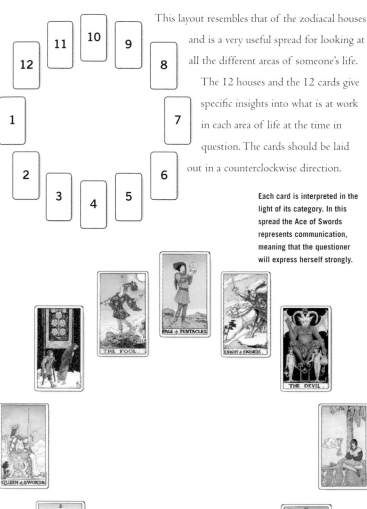

Each card is interpreted in the light of its category. In this spread the Ace of Swords represents communication, meaning that the questioner will express herself strongly.

Case history

GRACE

RECEPTIONIST

Grace, 35, came for a
Tarot reading because
she felt confused about
certain aspects of her life
and felt that she needed
some guidance. Although
she was not desperately
unhappy, she felt
unfulfilled in her life.

Position 1: Outer Personality ✦ The *Queen of Swords*
reflects Grace's intelligence, but suggests detachment.

Position 2: Values and Resources ✦ The *Two of Pentacles*
indicates that Grace has the talent, application, and
stamina to start something new and make a success of it.

Position 3: Communication ✦ The *Ace of Swords* suggests
Grace will experience a powerful new mental energy
and that clear thinking will help her to make decisions.

Position 4: Home and Family ✦ The *Hermit* highlights
her need for a period of reflection on her own.

Position 5: Creativity ✦ The *Magician* points to the fact
that Grace has reached a point in her life when she is
ready to develop her talents, skills, and creative abilities.

Position 6: Work ✦ The *Five of Wands* in this position is
telling Grace she is ready to test her skills in the market
place and compete with others to establish herself.

Position 7: Relationships ✦ The *Four of Cups* reflects the
fact that Grace is feeling dissatisfied in her marriage
and has a strong desire for some kind of change.

Position 8: Sexuality, Joint Resources ✦ The *Devil* shows
that Grace needs to confront the negative emotions she
is experiencing and bring them into the open.

Position 9: Spiritual Aspirations ✦ The *Knight of Swords*
indicates that Grace is ready to acquire a new
perspective but needs to broaden her horizons.

Position 10: Ambition, Career ✦ The *Page of Pentacles*
implies that Grace is ready to further her ambition,
perhaps by starting a training course or period of study.

Position 11: Aspirations ✦ The *Fool* in the eleventh
house suggests that Grace longs to make a fresh start.

Position 12: Unconscious Fears ✦ The *Five of Pentacles*
promises a new financial and emotional beginning.

The Triangle

```
  [5]     [4]
[6]  [ ]  [3]
    [1][2]
```

The Triangle is a useful spread for answering fairly specific questions, because it gives an overview of different influences. The first two cards address the present situation; the second two, the next few months; and the third two cards, the more long-term future. The central card, however, is the one to pay most attention to, because it carries most weight in a Tarot reading.

The seven-card Triangle spread is very useful for focusing on a specific issue. The central card often highlights both the current issue and the answer.

This spread gives the questioner an opportunity to focus on a particular problem that may be bothering them. In this case, the cards indicate an auspicious outcome.

Case history
SUSIE
ACCOUNTANT

Susie, 32, is married with a two-year-old child. Although she had a successful career, she felt it was the right time to have a second child. However, her husband had recently been laid off and she was now the sole breadwinner. She hoped that a reading would illuminate her dilemma.

Position 1 and 2: Present Situation ✦ The *Ten of Wands* suggests that Susie is feeling weighed down by too many responsibilities. She will not be in a position to start a new project until the load she bears has eased. *Justice* highlights the fact that she is facing a difficult decision that needs to be carefully weighed up. It is important that she holds onto what she believes in.

Positions 3 and 4: Immediate Future (the next 1–3 months) ✦ The *Lovers* is a card of change and implies that Susie is facing a choice that is neither easy nor straightforward. Her decision will involve a level of sacrifice. She needs to weigh up the pros and cons, as well as bear in mind that her intuition—not her intellect—is more likely to give her the "right" answer. The *Six of Swords* implies that Susie will soon be able to resolve her stressful situation and move into a calmer period. Although she will not find a solution overnight, the future definitely looks more hopeful.

Positions 5 and 6: Long-term future (the next 6–12 months) ✦ The *Empress* indicates that something in Susie's life will come to fruition and that her strong need for emotional well-being will be answered. The *Three of Cups* is the card of happiness and good fortune and indicates that there will be a joyful celebration within the next year. Susie can confidently look forward to the fulfillment of her heart's desire.

Position 7: Central card ✦ The *Sun* is an extremely optimistic card to choose, as it suggests that Susie has the energy and enthusiasm to fulfill her aspirations. Although she has been feeling below par, she will now start to feel more confident about the future. Joy and happiness in her marriage are also promised.

The Star Spread

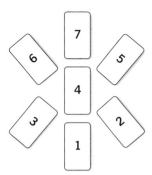

The Star is a seven-card layout, which gives a good overview of both the inner and outer influences of the questioner's life, as well as indicating the potential and the possibilities that are inherent at the time of the Tarot reading. For this spread it is possible to use just the Minor Arcana to understand the practical issues and the Major Arcana for a psychological overview.

The cards should be laid out following the diagram, starting from the center at the bottom. The final outcome is indicated by the topmost card.

This particular reading gives the questioner an in-depth look at what he needs to be aware of in order to find a more positive way forward.

Case history
ROB
BUSINESSMAN

Rob, 43, was recovering from a serious illness when he came for a reading. He had been a highly successful businessman, but was beginning to question why he had driven himself to the point of collapse. He wanted to change the pattern of his working life and was considering various options. Although somewhat apprehensive, he was contemplating going into therapy in order to understand himself better.

Position 1: Root of the Matter ✦ The *Ace of Wands* signifies that Rob is ready to embark on a new and inspiring phase of his life. Although this will necessitate hard work, this card suggests that it will be enjoyable, possibly leading to greater spiritual awareness.

Position 2: Emotional Life ✦ The *Seven of Cups* indicates that Rob feels many possibilities are opening up, but he must separate those ideas that are worth pursuing from those that are simply fantasy. This necessitates using his common sense to help him make a decision.

Position 3: Intellect and Working Life ✦ The *Page of Pentacles* suggests that Rob needs to be diligent and hard-working in his approach. Often this card indicates a period of study in order to further one's career. It underlines the fact that Rob feels that some personal development work will empower him in the workplace.

Position 4: Heart of the Matter ✦ The *Hierophant* reflects Rob's need to look deep within in order to find himself. It also mirrors his need to find a more meaningful context to his life. This card indicates that a teacher, therapist, or mentor may come into his life to guide him.

Position 5: Hopes and Fears ✦ The *Hanged Man* reflects Rob's fear about what he may have to sacrifice. At the same time, he hopes that making a life change will facilitate some kind of positive transformation.

Position 6: Conscious Desires ✦ The *Hermit* indicates that Rob needs to step back from his busy life and reflect. Time alone will bring him the insights he needs and help him to understand how to move forward.

Position 7: Outcome ✦ The *Six of Pentacles* is an excellent card to choose as the outcome, because it indicates that Rob's trust in life will be renewed.

The Consequences Spread

1	2	3
4	7	6
	5	

This seven-card layout is an extremely useful spread to undertake when the questioner has a difficult decision to make. It offers an overview of the situation (both in terms of past actions and current circumstances), as well as an indication of the immediate prospects, future actions, and the likely outcome. Often we are caught in the horns of a dilemma and find it hard to make a choice for fear of the consequences.

For this spread the cards are laid out in rows, starting from the top left-hand position and ending in the center.

This spread gives the questioner both encouragement and clarity and a sense that she will move forward in a meaningful direction.

Case history

MANDY

TEACHER

Mandy, 31, had just been given a promotion at work when her husband was offered a posting abroad. Although she felt quite excited by the idea of living abroad, she was reluctant to pass up the chance of getting ahead professionally.

Position 1: Current Circumstances ✦ The *Chariot* aptly describes the fact that Mandy feels pulled in two different directions. Her great desire to keep her job is matched by an equally ardent desire to live abroad. She needs to handle this dilemma with strength of mind.

Position 2: Immediate Prospects ✦ The *Eight of Wands* describes Mandy's option to live abroad. This card indicates that things are moving fast and that there is a growing momentum for change in her life.

Position 3: Past Actions ✦ The *Ace of Pentacles* suggests that Mandy had been able to secure a degree of material comfort and well-being and feels good about her own talents and the success she has achieved.

Position 4: Future Actions ✦ *Strength* suggests that Mandy has the stamina to cope with whatever is facing her. She needs to draw on her inner resources to resolve her current dilemma. This card also implies that she must consider whether she is acting in a selfish way.

Position 5: The Questioner's Potential ✦ The *Nine of Wands* indicates that Mandy is in a strong position to move forward in her life, although this card often signifies a setback before reaching the final goal.

Position 6: Outside Influences ✦ The *Knight of Wands* underlines the fact that travel is on the cards. It clearly reflects the fact that Mandy's life is going in a new direction. It also suggests considerable excitement at the prospect of change.

Position 7: Outcome ✦ The *Queen of Pentacles* as the outcome is a clear indication that, whatever transpires, Mandy will be feeling strong in herself and will have the opportunity to achieve something of real value. She is glad to realize that nothing will be lost.

The Five-Card Horseshoe Spread

This layout in the loose shape of a horseshoe gives a clear illustration of the questioner's present situation and desires, as well as a perspective on the future and a suggestion of the likely outcome. It can also reveal something that the questioner does not necessarily expect to hear, and is thus useful for understanding both what is evident and what is hidden from view in the questioner's life.

The cards are laid out in a semicircle, starting on the left and finishing on the right.

Although this questioner is feeling disaffected with certain aspects of his life, the reading suggests that things are more optimistic than he realizes.

Case history

PAUL

DESIGNER

Paul, 27, had been living with his girlfriend for three years at the time of the reading. He had been in the same job since he graduated and was beginning to feel as if his whole life was becoming stale. He was hoping that the reading would give him some direction and would highlight his current malaise.

Position 1: Present Position ✦ The *Two of Swords* reflects the fact that Paul feels in a rut, but is unable to make a move because of fear of the consequences. He does not want to lose his girlfriend or his job and is in conflict with himself. He needs to be very honest if he is going to be able to take action and move his life forward.

Position 2: Present Desires ✦ The *Two of Wands* indicates that, although Paul is reluctant to make a decision, on some level he is in fact ready to choose what to do next. He is hoping that new opportunities will present themselves, but this card suggests that he will have to take the initiative. Both a career decision and a resolution about his relationship need to be made.

Position 3: The Unexpected ✦ The *Nine of Cups* reveals that, despite Paul's ambivalence about committing himself to his girlfriend, the promise of true happiness is in the offing. This card indicates contentment in love, and suggests a happy marriage and emotional and material security. Paul needs to follow his heart, and not his intellect, in making his decision.

Position 4: Immediate Future ✦ The *Knight of Cups* reinforces the message of the previous card, and indicates that the spirit of romance is being evoked. A proposal of marriage is being shown, although this card stresses the importance of considering all the implications before making a commitment.

Position 5: Outcome ✦ The *Ten of Pentacles* indicates a very positive outcome for Paul. It suggests a feeling of well-being and security. This is a very auspicious card to choose for starting a family or any kind of business venture, and signifies that Paul will have the emotional and financial resources for this new phase in his life.

Creating your own spread

| 1 | 2 | 3 |

Creating your own spread is a very good way to develop your confidence in reading the cards and to deepen your understanding of them.

You can create a spread of your own and tailor-make it to your personal situation. All you need to do is decide on the layout and what each card will represent. For example, if you have a major decision to make (such as whether to move house), you could choose a simple three-card spread that indicates the way forward, whatever is helping or hindering you in the process, and the final outcome or resolution. If the reading is inconclusive, you might need to introduce more categories to give you a fuller picture of the forces at work in your particular circumstances.

With just three categories you can gain invaluable experience of synthesizing the meaning of the cards in order to give a coherent overview.

Case history

FIONA

HOUSEWIFE

Here is a spread that I did for Fiona, 37, who was in conflict with her family over a house move. She was very keen to move to the country, but the rest of her family was resolute in wanting to stay in London. She wanted to know if she should force the issue or should go with the general consensus.

Position 1: The Way Forward ✦ The *Five of Swords* in this position shows that Fiona feels powerless to do anything about the current impasse and that ultimately she will have to concede defeat and give up on her hope of moving to the country. This card suggests that it will be hard for her to accept the constrictions imposed on her, but that she has no choice but to swallow her pride and back off. She will undoubtedly experience this as a loss, but she needs to face the situation honestly and accept that now is not the right time for a change.

Position 2: Help/Hindrance ✦ *The Moon* implies that Fiona is prone to self-deception and illusion. This card often indicates a sense of depression and hopelessness and an inability to see the way forward. Certainly this is how Fiona is feeling. However, on a more positive note, it also reflects the fact that Fiona is ready to develop her intuition more fully and gain insight into herself. This will help her to understand the deeper motivations for wanting to move and how she can best address them.

Position 3: Outcome ✦ *Judgement* as the outcome of Fiona's situation points to the fact that she needs to let go of some aspect of her past so that she can experience a new lease of life. She is being given an opportunity to take an honest look at her situation and evaluate how true to herself she has been in the past. She now realizes that there are certain things that she needs to resolve before she will be in a postion to make a fresh start—this is the underlying reason why she is being stopped from moving on at this point in time. In the future, things could look different.

Useful websites and books

WEBSITES

American Tarot Association
http://www.ata-tarot.com/
A useful website for Tarot students, teachers, and masters

Canadian Tarot Network
http://www.tarotcanada.com/
For those who are interested in the Tarot and willing to maintain high moral standards

International Tarot Society
http://www.geocities.com/Athens/Ithaca/3772/
Sets out to improve Tarot practice and to sponsor courses

Introduction to the Tarot
denvid@poetic.com
Information and advice on Tarot by email

Jungian Tarot Course
entrance@icon.co.za
Also supplies information and advice by email

Learning the Tarot
http://www.kasamba.com/
Everything the Tarot novice needs to know

Learning the Tarot On-line
http://www2.dgsys.com/~bunning/top.html
A Tarot course consisting of 19 lessons

Tarot Classes
http://www.tarotschool.com/
Classes that may be done either on-line or by correspondence

Tarot Directory
http://tarotfool.com
A useful website offering advice on how to get started

Tarot Discussions
http://www.facade.com/attraction/tarot
Discussions on Tarot-related matters, including how it originated

Tarot and Healing
http://www.angelpaths.com
Explores the use of the Tarot in healing

Tarot and Kabbalah
http://members.ficom.net/ditch/tarot.htm
Explores the link between the Hebrew Kabbalah and the Tarot

Tarot Mailing List
http://www.lightspeed.bc.ca/hilander/tarotl.html
A mailing list for participatory discussion on all aspects of the Tarot

Tarot and Palmistry Readings
http://www.jfinternational.com/psy/homepage_psychic.htm
Readings that combine palmistry, the Tarot, and astrology

Tarot News and Reviews
http://www.nccn.net/~tarot/
News, reviews, and other information

Tarot Readings Online
http://www.tarothaven.com/
The best Tarot readings

Tarot Superstore
http://www.search.freefind.com
Sells a range of Tarot items, with secure ordering facilities

US Games Systems, Inc.
http://www.usgamesinc.com
Sells a huge range of Tarot decks, plus playing cards and games

BOOKS

Almond, Jocelyn, and Seddon, Keith
Tarot for Relationships
Aquarian Press, 1990

Banzhaf, Hajo
The Tarot Handbook
US Games Systems, Inc., 1993

Crowley, Aleister
The Book of Thoth
US Games Systems, 1977

Decker, Ronald, Depaulis, Thierry,
and Dummett, Michael
A Wicked Pack of Cards
St. Martin's Press, 1996

Douglas, Alfred
The Tarot: The Origins, Meaning, and Uses
Penguin, 1972

Dummett, Michael
The Game of Tarot
US Games Systems, 1980

Gray, Eden
Complete Guide to the Tarot
Bantam, 1971

Greer, Mary K.
Tarot for Yourself
Newcastle, 1984

Kaplan, Stuart R.
The Encyclopedia of Tarot, vols. 1, 2, 3
US Games Systems, Inc., 1978

Knight, Gareth
The Magical World of Tarot
Aquarian Press, 1992

Mathers, S. L.
Tarot
Gordon, 1973

Moakley, Gertrude
The Tarot Cards Painted by
Bonifacio Bembo
New York Public Library, 1966

Noble, Vicki
Motherpeace: A Way to the Goddess
Through Myth, Art, and Tarot
Harper and Row, 1983

Norman, Marsha
The Fortune Teller
Random House, 1987

O'Neill, Robert V.
Tarot Symbolism
Fairways Press, 1986

Peach, Emily
The Tarot Workbook
Aquarian Press, 1984

Pollack, Rachel
Tarot Readings and Meditations
Aquarian Press, 1990

Riley, Jana
Tarot Dictionary and
Compendium
Samuel Weiser, 1995

Sharman-Burke, Juliet
Understanding the Tarot
Rider, 1998

Waite, A. E.
The Pictorial Key to the Tarot
Samuel Weiser, 1983

Wang, Robert
Quabalistic Tarot
Samuel Weiser, 1983

Ziegler, Gerd
Tarot: The Mirror of the Soul
Samuel Weiser, 1988

Index

A

Apollo   11
archetypes   13, 17, 19, 38
Arthur, King   66

B

Berrill, Roland   8

C

cartomancy   13
case histories   187–203
Celtic Cross   189–9
Chariot   8, 14, 34–5
Clubs   94
Coins   122, 138, 146
Consequences
  Spread   198–9
Cronus   38
Crowley, Aleister   8
Cups   7, 65, 66–93

D

Death   14, 46–7
Devil   50–1
Disks   122, 144

E

Emperor   6, 28–9
Empress   8, 18, 26–7

F

Five-Card Horseshoe
  Spread   200–1
Fool   7, 8, 19, 20–1
friend, reading for a   186

G

Golden Dawn Tarot   6, 8
  Cups   67, 73, 80, 85, 90
  Major Arcana   27, 42, 62
  Pentacles   122, 133, 139,
                    145, 148
  Swords   153, 165, 172
  Wands   103, 111, 114,
                    115, 121

H

Hanged Man   18, 44–5
Herbal Tarot   18
  Cups   69, 77, 82, 93
  Major Arcana   43, 52
  Pentacles   122, 123, 128,
                 133, 141, 147
  Swords   151, 163, 169,
                           176
  Wands   98, 99, 109, 111
Hermit   18, 38–9
Hierophant   8, 30–1
High Priest   11, 14
High Priestess   11, 24–5
history   10–11
Hobdell, Michael   8
Holy Grail   66, 88
Horoscope Spread   192–3

J

Judgment   60–1
Jung, Carl   12, 38, 62
Justice   18, 36–7

L

Lovers   10, 32–3
Lucifer   50

M

Magician   22–3
Major Arcana   7, 11, 14,
            19–63, 64, 181, 185
Marseilles Tarot   8, 10
  Cups   75, 82, 83, 88
  Major Arcana   20, 25,
                    35, 40, 51
  Pentacles   149
  readings   180
  Swords   150, 161, 167,
                           170
  Wands   101, 107, 118
Medieval Scapini Tarot   18
  Cups   71, 89
  Major Arcana   21, 38,
                      58, 63

Pentacles   127, 132, 141,
                    146, 147
  Swords   157, 166, 177
  Wands   98, 105, 110,
                           121
Minor Arcana   7, 11, 14,
                       65–186
Moon   58–9
Morgan Greer Tarot   18
  Cups   67, 74, 81, 84, 89
  Major Arcana   28, 33, 4
                      5, 48
  Pentacles   125, 131,
                    136, 143
  Swords   150, 151, 159,
                 162, 167, 173
  Wands   95, 100, 103,
            110, 111, 112, 119
Mythic Tarot   180

P

Papess   11, 24–5
Pentacles   7, 65, 122–49
Pierpont Morgan Visconti-
  Sforza Tarot   8, 10
  Cups   66, 75, 80, 81
  Major Arcana   23, 30,
                      50, 59
  Pentacles   125, 137, 149
  Swords   156, 163,
                 171, 174
  Wands   96, 109, 115
Plato   34
Pope   11, 30–1

R

readings 179–86
Rods 94
Royal Fez Moroccan Tarot 8
Cups 76, 85, 91
Major Arcana 36, 39, 54
Pentacles 124, 131, 138,
139, 142
Swords 154, 160, 161, 169
Wands 97, 106, 107,
108, 116
Russian Tarot
of St. Petersburg 18
Cups 72, 83, 91
Major Arcana 26, 53, 60
Pentacles 129, 138
Swords 153, 158,
165, 175
Wands 99, 106, 117

S

Satan 50
scene-setting 182–3
Sforza, Francesco 10
Shakov, Yuri 18
spreads 185, 187–203
Star 54–5
Star Spread 196–7
Strength 42–3
Sun 56–7
Swiss IJJ Tarot 18
Cups 69, 79, 87, 93

Major Arcana 29, 44,
56, 61
Pentacles 123, 129,
135, 146
Swords 155, 176, 177
Wands 94, 105, 113, 114
Swords 7, 65, 150–77
symbolism 10–11,
14–15, 181
synchronicity 12, 184–5

T

Temperance 18, 48–9
Thoth Tarot 8
Cups 70, 73, 79, 86
Major Arcana 22, 31,
46, 57
Pentacles 127, 130,
135, 144
readings 180
Swords 155, 160,
170, 171
Wands 97, 104, 120
Three-Card Spread 190–1
Tower 52–3
Triangle Spread 194–5

U

Ukiyoe Tarot 180
Universal Waite Tarot 8,
178, 180
Cups 71, 78, 87, 92
Major Arcana 24, 34,
41, 55
Pentacles 134, 140,
145
Swords 152, 156, 157,
168, 174, 175
Wands 102, 113
Universe 12, 62

V

Visconti, Bianca Maria 10

W

Waite, Arthur 8
Wands 7, 65, 94–121
Wheel of Fortune 40–1
Witches Tarot 180
World 16, 62–3

Z

Zodiac 8
Zolar's Astrological
Tarot 18
Cups 68, 77
Major Arcana 37, 49
Pentacles 126, 137, 143
Swords 159, 164,
172, 173
Wands 100, 101,
118, 119

Acknowledgments

TAROT CARDS

Illustrations from the Aleister Crowley Thoth
Tarot by permission of OTO, Ordo Templi
Orientis International/© OTO.
Further reproduction prohibited.

Illustrations from the following Tarot
decks are reproduced by permission of
US Games Systems, Inc., 17 Ludlow Street,
Stamford, CT 06902, USA.
Further reproduction prohibited.

Cary Yale Visconti Tarot © 1985
Golden Dawn Tarot © 1982
Herbal Tarot © 1990
Medieval Scapini Tarot © 1985
Morgan Greer Tarot © 1993
Oswald Wirth Tarot © 1976
Pierpoint Morgan Visconti-Sforza Tarot © 1975
Royal Fez Moroccan Tarot © 1975
Russian Tarot of St. Petersburg © 1996
Ukiyoe Tarot © 1983
Universal Waite Tarot © 1990
Zolar's Astrological Tarot © 1983

Illustrations from the Swiss 1JJ Tarot deck
reproduced by permission of US Games
Systems, Inc., Stamford, CT 06902/AG Muller,
Neuhausen am Rheinfall, Switzerland.
Copyright © 1974 by US Games Systems/
AG Muller. Further reproduction prohibited.

Illustrations from the Tarot of Marseilles
deck reproduced by permission
of US Games Systems, Inc., Stamford,
CT 06902/Carta Mundi, Turnhout, Belgium.
Copyright © 1996 by US Games
Systems/Carta Mundi.
Further reproduction prohibited.